"Friendship is the source of the greatest pleasures, and without friends even the most agreeable pursuits become tedious."

Thomas Aquinas[1]

Copyright

ISBN 978-1-952359-31-6   (paperback)
ISBN 978-1-952359-36-1   (ebook)

For More Information
About the Life Planning Series:

www.lifeplanningtools.com

Life Planning Series
by J. S. Wellman

CHOOSE
Friends Wisely

Make authentic personal connections.

LIFE PLANNING SERIES
J.S. WELLMAN

Extra-mile Publishing

Free PDF

Wise
Decision-Making

[Get the ebook version for 99 cents]

We want to give you a <u>free</u> copy of:

Wise Decision-Making:
You can make good choices.

This book will help you make good
decisions in your life, career, family . . .

Free PDF:
www.lifeplanningtools.link/howtodecide

eBook for 99 cents:
https://www.amazon.com/dp/B09SYGWRVL/

Ebook

Free PDF

Improve your life!
Life Planning Handbook

Obtain a copy of the Handbook if you want to be guided in developing your own personal Life Plan.

Purpose of a Life Plan

- To help you develop direction in your life.
- To encourage you to make good decisions.
- To help build your life on proven life principles.
- To help you establish goals for your life.
- To identify what you hope to accomplish in life.
- To help you make the most of every opportunity.

Life Planning Series

Life Planning Handbook

Go to www.amazon.com/dp/1952359325
to get your copy now.

Don't wait to have a better life!

Table of Contents

	Page
Copyright	2
Title Page	3
Wise Decision-making	4
Life Planning Handbook	5
Table of Contents	6
Message From the Author	8
Life Planning Series	10
Prelude	14

CHAPTER 1 - INTRODUCTION

Core Values and Principles	16
Personal Growth	18
Tips For Overcoming Barriers	21

CHAPTER 2 – CONSEQUENCES

General	23
There Will be Consequences	24
The Slacker	25
Count the Cost	26
Envy	27
Legacy	28
We Reap What We Sow	30
It's Not Fair	32
Who To Blame	33
Mistakes	34
Tips	35

CHAPTER 3 – FRIENDS LIFE PRINCIPLE	37
CHAPTER 4 – WHO IS YOUR FRIEND?	43
CHAPTER 5 – HOW DO FRIENDS ACT?	49
CHAPTER 6 – CHOOSE FRIENDS WISELY	64

CHAPTER 7 – HOW TO ACQUIRE FRIENDS   73

CHAPTER 8 – FRIENDSHIP REQUIREMENTS   83

CHAPTER 9 – BE A FRIEND TO GAIN A FRIEND   88

CHAPTER 10 – PLANNING PART 1: Life Analysis   94
    [Know Yourself]

CHAPTER 11 – PLANNING PART 2: Life Values   104
    [Core Values, Priorities, Commitments]

CHAPTER 12 – PLANNING PART 3: Life Goals
    Friends Life Principle   116

CHAPTER 13 – PLANNING PART 4: Action Steps   118

CHAPTER 14 – PLANNING PART 5:
    Ongoing Progress Review   132

CHAPTER 15 – IMPLEMENTATION TECHNIQUES   134

APPENDIX A – HOW TO PRIORITIZE   135
APPENDIX B – DECISION-MAKING   137
APPENDIX C – COACHING ASSISTANCE   141
APPENDIX D – CHECK LIST   143

Next Steps   145
Life Planning Series Books   148
Wise Decision-Making   150
Life Planning Handbook   151
Acknowledgements   152
Notes   153
About Author   156
Contact Us   157
Make a Difference   158

Message From Author

The general purpose of this book and the Life Planning Series is to encourage you to pursue actions and character traits that will produce your best life. The book series will address 15 to 25 significant activities or traits that help people improve their lives and live a better life.

First, understand that you can improve or acquire high personal character and outstanding habits, no matter how good or bad your life may be at this moment. Good personal character and good life habits <u>can be</u> achieved. They will allow you to live a better life.

Second, know that you don't have to read all the books in this series to make a significant change or improvement in your life. Find the books that focus on the areas of your life that you want to improve.

Third, know that this is a progressive journey. You don't need to climb the highest mountain immediately. You may just want to learn more about the basic principles of good character. This series will provide you with a foundation for decisions relative to your lifestyle, goals, priorities, and commitments.

Fourth, know that the key to developing high character and making good decisions in your life is *intentionality*. The Life Planning Series will help you identify the path you want to travel, but you will need to be intentional about walking that path if you want to make progress toward the goal of living a better life.

Fifth, know that change will require making good decisions, establishing important core values in your life, setting priorities, and making commitments. This book will help you identify the values in life that will produce high personal character and good habits.

Sixth, know that this series, and the entire Life Planning product line, are designed to help you smooth out the path for your life journey. We will provide the tools you need to make the best choices and decisions for traveling your life path.

Seventh, remember that all actions (both words and deeds) have consequences. These consequences will impact you and all those around you. Read carefully Chapter 2 on "Consequences," which is particularly important for your understanding when making decisions.

Lastly, the very simple formula for success is: "*Decide you want to do it and work at it regularly*."

This book will give you guidance and we will even provide coaching if you want it. If you want to improve your life, just commit and carry through. We are here to help!

Decide to be the very best you can be!

Life Planning Series

Before you read this book it will be useful if you have an understanding of the purpose and focus of the entire Life Planning Series. The series will examine major personal characteristics, traits, and habits that are fundamental influencers in life. Each book will include a Life Analysis focused on the subject of the book and then help you develop a plan to improve *that particular area* in your life. In addition, we can provide coaching assistance for those who want hands-on help.

Those who want to develop a *total life plan* can do that by acquiring our *Life Planning Handbook*. For more details, see the "Next Steps" section at the end of this book and the Ad Page describing the book following that section.

LIFE PLANNING SERIES

It is our objective in these books to help you choose the best path and give you tools to make good decisions in your life journey. The series is divided into five different categories to help organize the books and make it easy for you to find related subjects.

All the books will be meaningful to a general reading audience, but because the Christian viewpoint brings a different approach to many of these subjects and concepts, that perspective will be addressed in a separate Christian Wisdom Series. That series is intended for Christians but others may find the first book in that series particularly interesting because it is focused on the proverbs of the Bible. The Christian Wisdom Series will be published after the Life Planning Series is complete.

The initial plan is to publish books on the following topics:

Subjects		Life Principle
Personal Character:		
Integrity*	honesty, truth, compromise/standing firm, justice, fairness	Be honest, live with integrity, and base Life on truth.
Reputation	respect, responsibility, sincerity	Earn the respect of others.
Leadership	power, decisiveness, courage, influence, loyalty	Lead well and be a loyal follower.
Identity/Self-Image	humor, being genuine, authenticity, confidence	Be confident in who you are.
Wisdom	discernment, correction, folly, foolishness	Seek knowledge, understanding, and wisdom.
Personal Relationships:		
Friends*	Friends, associates, acquaintances	Choose your friends wisely.
Family	Honor, parenting, discipline	Honor your family.
Love	Love is . . .	Love one another.
Compassion	humility, mercy, goodness, kindness	Treat others as you would want to be treated.
Forgiveness	reject grudges and revenge	Forgive others; do not hold grudges or take revenge.

Self-Control:

Speech*		Guard your speech.
Anger	self-control, self-discipline, patience	Always be under control.
Addiction	moderation, life balance	Live a life of balance and moderation, not excess.
Immorality	temptation	Set high moral standards.

Work Ethic:

Diligence*	apathy, laziness, perseverance, resilience, energy	Be diligent and a hard worker.
Trustworthiness	dependability, reliability, responsibility	Be trustworthy, dependable, and reliable.
Skills	curiosity, knowledge, education, abilities	Seek excellence; strive to do everything well.

Wealth:

Money*	wealth, poverty	Make sound financial choices.
Gratitude	generosity, thankfulness, gratefulness	Be thankful, grateful, and generous.

*The first subject listed under each of the categories above make up the Primary Life Principles.

After the initial launch of the first five books in the series, the books will be published in 4 to 8 week intervals.

LIFE PLANNING HANDBOOK

The purpose of this book is to produce a total and complete Life Plan for all the major activities in your life:

1. Life Principles and Character Attributes
2. Habits
3. Friends and Family Relationships
4. Work and Work Ethic
5. Education
6. Community Service
7. Money and Wealth
8. Health
9. Spiritual

The planning process in this book will examine your skills and abilities, your personal life values, core values, priorities, and commitments. The book will help you identify your life goals and create action steps to achieve those goals. It also includes additional help and tools in the Appendix. Coaching assistance is available for those who want additional help.

These products and services will generate purpose, direction, and growth in your life.

Choose the subjects and products that work for you and your needs.

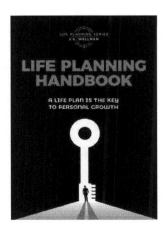

PRELUDE

"Character is like a tree and reputation like its shadow.
The shadow is what we think of it;
the tree is the real thing."
Abraham Lincoln[2]

The primary purpose of this book is to inform, encourage, and inspire readers to choose good friends wisely. We can learn a wealth of practical wisdom for daily living from common sense, wise sayings, logical thinking, and quotes from wise people.

The second and equally important purpose is to help you develop a plan that will assist you in implementing change in your life. The latter portion of this book is an easy-to-follow planning process for implementing that change.

The third purpose is our hope that you will pass it on. It is our desire that you will not only obtain this knowledge, but pass it on to others – particularly friends, children, grandchildren, or students.

An African proverb says, *"Don't spend all day rejoicing on your bench. When you pray, move your feet!"* The message of this proverb is that if you want to accomplish something, that will not happen if you're sitting on your bench all day. Growth and improvement, including living a better life, require action and intentionality. The good news is that you can use the information in this book and in the Life Planning Series to acquire knowledge that will help you follow a path to a better life.

Intentionality with a plan is the foundation for making progress!

Chapter 1

INTRODUCTION

Know your core values,
because they will drive your life.

CORE VALUES OF THE LIFE PLANNING SERIES

The Life Planning products are developed around the following ten core values and principles:

1. Wise sayings, parables, proverbs, common sense, and street smarts provide an underlying foundation for gaining knowledge, understanding, and wisdom.

2. Honesty, integrity, and living a life based on truth are the foundational character traits for achieving a life of hope and contentment. They are the cornerstones to living a better life.

3. There are five <u>Primary</u> Life Principles:

- be honest, live with integrity, and base your life on truth,
- choose your friends wisely,
- choose your words carefully,
- be a diligent and hard worker, and
- do not love money or worship wealth.

4. Life change is possible. You can make positive changes and expect good results to follow. All choices have consequences.

5. It is not necessary to change a large number of character traits in order to achieve significant life improvement. Changing a few key areas can have a major impact on your quality of life.

6. The key to making any life change is *intentionality*.

7. Perfection is not possible, but if we aim for it, we can achieve significant results. Nothing will be attained if we do not try.

8. We will be open about the difficulties, barriers, and walls that one might experience in implementing life change. But barriers can be torn down.

9. The ultimate purpose in this series is to develop an effective plan for improving life circumstances. It is not our intent to provide lengthy textbooks on the particular subjects. Our presentation of the text material will be limited to what you need to know in order to develop an effective plan to improve your life.

10. Life is a progressive journey requiring good choices and a solid foundation for the future. Time is needed to implement change. Patience and perseverance will be necessary to achieve the desired results.

CUSTOMER CHARACTERISTICS

The ideal readers for our Life Planning products are people who:

- want to learn more about the subject of personal growth and self-improvement,

- want to live a good life, live at peace, be content, or have a successful life,
- want to dig more deeply into the meaning of living a good life,
- may be confused, have a history of bad choices, or are living in chaos,
- are feeling overwhelmed or discouraged,
- desire to change or improve their life, or
- want to learn how to make good or better decisions.

PERSONAL GROWTH

We will encourage you to make good choices and improve your life. This process is often referred to as personal growth. Some might call it self-help. However you think of it, our objective is to help you improve your life through the use of widely accepted life principles.

There are many good reasons for pursuing personal growth in life. We have already mentioned several in the preceding pages. Here are a few more:

- to find personal peace, meaning, and purpose;
- to gain more control over life circumstances;
- to be more effective in certain skills, abilities or decisions;
- to become more disciplined;
- to change an attitude or overcome a negative outlook;
- to expand potential horizons;
- to open new avenues of understanding; and
- to change certain outcomes in your life.

For the purpose of living your best life, you may only need help focusing on the right things. You may just need guidance in finding things you can tweak to make a few changes in your lifestyle. You may want a clearer vision of your goals. Or you may want to do some serious work on some particular aspect of your life. Our Life Planning products will help you achieve any of these desires.

BARRIERS TO PERSONAL GROWTH

Our commitment to the truth requires that we point out possible barriers that would keep you from achieving a better life. They can be overcome if you are intentional, but understand that you may encounter the following barriers:

- APATHY: You are not a self-starter and you tend to lack discipline. You are generally comfortable with your present life and find change frightening. Your commitment level is not high and change may seem to be too much work.

  Intentionality is the key to overcoming apathy. The starting point is desire. You must want to make something happen. The solution is to say "yes" to change and allow this book to guide your thoughts and actions toward living a better life.

- BUSY LIFE: You are too busy. You have no time. Your calendar is already too full.

  This reason comes up again and again as a serious deterrent to achieving any goal.

People are just extremely busy today. Life is too full. We are trying to find happiness and joy in doing things. We never stop to think, reflect, or meditate on life. Being too busy and the unwise use of our time are the biggest hurdles for completing any task. The solution is to change your priorities and your calendar.

- FEAR: You are afraid of taking risk, you fear embarrassment, or you are afraid you don't have the necessary skills to achieve any meaningful results. You are afraid it won't really work and you will have invested time that will be lost. You may be afraid to admit you need help!

  If you fear that it might not work we would encourage you to look at it in a more positive way. The solution is to think about what might be possible if you commit to this as passionately as you work at the other things you love.

- PEER PRESSURE: You might be considered a loser and be shunned by your group if they found out.

  It is true that peer pressure can be very hard to deal with. If you discover that your core values are in conflict with those of your friends and associates, you will ultimately face some difficult decisions. A better life will be lived when your core values match those of your close friends, particularly in the important areas of character, ethics, and moral standards. The solution is to choose your friends carefully.

20

Yes, there are barriers, but they can be overcome. The purpose of the Life Planning Series is to address important areas of life that are worthy of your time and effort. Again, there can be barriers, and you should be aware of them so you can determine how to overcome them.

Barriers can be overcome and torn down!

TIPS FOR OVERCOMING BARRIERS

Difficulties and barriers can be overcome if you want to find a solution. It's a lot easier to make changes in life if you are not doing it alone or if you are receiving guidance and help. In addition to our books and products we suggest finding someone to join you in your quest for a better life. If you cannot find someone to participate with you, find someone you can meet with weekly or periodically to discuss your progress, your difficulties, your needs, and most of all your successes.

Here are six effective ways to overcome barriers:

1. Recognize that many barriers are just excuses.
2. Recruit a support person (true friend) to hold you accountable (meet once a week).
3. Recruit others to do it with you. Push each other.
4. Do not expect change, improvement, or miracles overnight.
5. Recruit support and understanding from your family (spouse, children, or siblings).
6. If time is a hurdle – work it out. Adjust your priorities.

Alternatively, we will provide personal coaching for any parts of the plan. See Appendix C at the end of this book for information about our Coaching Assistance.

LUCK

Don't place any hope in luck. Generally luck has very little to do with favorable or unfavorable results. You can get lucky and win the lottery, but your abilities, skills, and strengths are not the result of luck. Yes, you can have God-given skills and abilities, but much of what you accomplish in life is the result of hard work and diligence, not luck.

Our lives will be the result of decisions we make and the consequences of those decisions. If you decide you want to be a plumber and you go to school and get the proper training and then intern with a licensed plumber, it is not luck that after ten years you have a successful plumbing business. The success was the result of planning, hard work, and dedication to a goal.

TIPS YOU COULD USE

a. Underline, circle, or highlight the 1 to 3 tips above that you think could make the most impact if you implemented them in your life. You will revisit these choices at the end of the book in the Planning section.

b. There may be other things that you think would make a difference. Write them below:

_____

_____

_____

_____

In reality barriers are just excuses!

Chapter 2

CONSEQUENCES

"Mess with the bull and one usually gets the horns."
Latin American saying[3]

GENERAL

Consequences are a vital concept in our understanding of making good choices and setting goals to have a successful life. Thus, this chapter on consequences will appear in each of the books in the Life Planning Series. You have complete freedom to choose what you want to do. But, you cannot choose the consequences. Thus, it is important to manage and control your actions because the result of poor choices could be a disaster.

You and I will bear the consequences of our words and actions. It is like a law of nature. My wife drilled this concept into our kids. If she said it once she said it a thousand times, "Your actions all have consequences." And, when she said it, the kids knew there was no "eventually" involved.

If you don't want to endure the negative results of poor decisions, think in advance what your actions are likely to produce. What you do and what you say will have lasting impact on others and on yourself.

THERE WILL BE CONSEQUENCES

Life is a series of decisions and choices. We are constantly making choices about both significant and insignificant situations. The advice above is a good example of the importance of consequences. Choices shape the course of our lives. Some people learn a great deal from the consequences of their actions and others seem oblivious and never learn anything.

You may hear some people claim that their actions do not have consequences. This is absolutely not true. Consequences are real and can produce both good and bad results. Our goal is to help you make better choices and deal with the consequences.

Physical consequences are a law of nature. If you touch a hot stove you will get burned. If you walk into the street in front of a truck you will be injured. Behaviors have predictable consequences as well. If you cheat and lie, people will stop doing business with you and your reputation will suffer. If you are not dependable, people will learn not to trust you.

We know of a person who had surgery and was told not to walk on his repaired knee. He ignored the doctor's orders and hobbled around on crutches anyway. He lost his balance, fell through a glass door, and received additional injuries. He blamed the doctor for an outcome that was clearly the consequence of his own poor choice.

By definition consequences occur as a result of something else happening. They are the outcome of some other action. The result may occur immediately or it could take a while, even years. This is often one of the reasons that we make poor choices – the consequence does not occur immediately and because of this we think there will never be consequences. We cannot allow this delay to persuade us that consequences don't happen.

The actual consequences you experience will vary depending on your circumstances, but there will be consequences nonetheless. The degree or size of the consequence will also vary, but we should not be fooled into thinking small transgressions are insignificant. Even seemingly small acts can produce significant consequences.

> *"One who steals has no right*
> *to complain if he is robbed."*
> Aesop[4]

THE SLACKER

There was a farmer who had been plowing hard for many days with an ox and mule yoked together. The ox told the mule that they should pretend to be sick and rest. The mule declined saying, "No, we must get the work done, for the season is short." But the ox played sick and the farmer brought him hay and corn and made him comfortable.

When the mule came in from plowing the ox asked how things had gone. The mule said, "We didn't get as much done but we did okay, I guess." The ox asked, "Did the old man say anything about me?" Nothing," said the mule. The next day the ox played sick again. When the tired mule came in he asked again how it went. "All right, but we sure didn't get much done." The ox asked, "What did the old man say about me?" The mule replied, "Nothing directly to me, but he had a long talk with the butcher."[5]

This is similar to the message in the old story concerning the consequences of a hearty breakfast to the chicken and the pig. A breakfast of ham and eggs to the chicken is a temporary inconvenience, but to the pig it is a permanent and lasting consequence – it's a <u>real</u> commitment.

You will need to make a real commitment in order to claim the Friends Life Principle as a foundational truth in your life. You may find it tempting to be lazy, particularly if no one is looking over your shoulder. However, sooner or later that behavior will catch up with you.

We chose the word "slacker" as the heading for this story although it is typically not used today. It means someone who avoids his work or obligations. The synonyms for slacker may surprise you: no-account, vagrant, good-for-nothing, and bum. If you tend to get a little lazy with your undertakings, remember the ox in this story. The projected destination for the ox was not a desirable result. You cannot afford to be lazy or apathetic when it comes to how well you are going to live life.

All actions have consequences!

COUNT THE COST

Someone has said that you will ultimately be invited to a party where you will dine on your own consequences. Whether your actions were wise or unwise, you will eventually bear the consequences. Thus, it is important to think about the consequences in advance and count the cost. What will result from your words or actions?

If you don't want to endure the negative results of poor choices, think in advance what your actions are likely to produce. What will you say when co-workers urge you to join them at the local bar every night before you go home?

What will you say if someone makes a sexual advance or lurid remark? What will you do or say if you are offered some form of drug? What will you do or say if someone who has been drinking offers you a ride home? What will you do if you are encouraged to cheat or lie?

Regardless of the particular situation, it will always be easier to arrive at a positive outcome if you have thought ahead, evaluated the circumstances, and determined in advance how you will respond to these types of situations.

What you do and say in questionable circumstances will have a lasting impact on your life. This truth is almost as important as understanding that the world is round and not flat. Emblazon the following truth in your mind and on your heart:

Consequences shape lives.
Choices produce consequences
which direct the course of life.
Therefore, count the cost!

ENVY

The Oxford Dictionary describes envy as a feeling of discontented or resentful longing aroused by someone else's possessions, qualities, luck, or situation. Envy is not an attractive attribute. You may think the grass is greener in that other field but it may not be as attractive as you think. Buddha has said:

"Do not overrate what you have received,
nor envy others. He who envies others
does not obtain peace of mind."
Buddha[6]

27

There is no purpose or peace in envy. Coveting the things of others, whether they are material objects, mental abilities, or acquired skills, will not produce anything worthwhile. Honoré de Balzac has said, "Envy is the most stupid of vices, for there is no single advantage to be gained from it."[7] He is absolutely right! I challenge you to think of a positive attribute of envy.

Consider the following questions:

- Why do you want it? Is it something you need or simply want?

- Envy implies jealousy, covetousness, and resentment. Which of these is driving your envy?

- If you acquire the object of your envy, what are you going to do with it? Why?

It is certainly appropriate to admire people of character and status. It is also appropriate to desire and copy their good habits and character traits. But that's not envy.

Determine what you want and define your goals in terms of what you want your life to be. Don't waste time resenting or desiring that what your neighbor has.

LEGACY

Our words and actions can have impact for a long time. The ongoing impact of poor behavior is a concept that escapes many people. Poor decisions can affect a family for many generations. Bad behavior establishes a pattern that becomes the blueprint for a child's future behavior.

For example, parents who frequently lie are modeling lying as an acceptable way to avoid responsibility, inherently teaching their children that lying and deception are acceptable ways of behaving.

What children experience become their normal responses in similar situations. What is witnessed by small children is later reproduced. They can learn to be trustworthy, reliable, and dependable, or they can learn to do drugs, smoke, and gossip. What a child sees modeled in his home becomes his normal response, and that behavior cycle continues into future generations.

Your actions, both good and bad, establish the foundation of your life, lifestyle, and legacy.

Your legacy extends into future generations; therefore, be sure that it is a positive one! Most people have no concept of how their behavior can impact the future. This is dramatically demonstrated by comparing the lives of Jonathan Edwards and Max Jukes.

Jonathan Edwards was a Puritan preacher in the 1700s. His descendants demonstrate the powerful influence of wise choices and a godly life. At the turn of the 20th century, A. E. Winship decided to trace the descendants of Jonathan Edwards and compare them to a man known as Max Jukes.

Mr. Jukes was incarcerated in the New York prison system at the time Jonathan Edwards was preaching. Winship found that 42 of the men in the New York prison system could trace their heritage back to Max Jukes. Jukes, an atheist, lived a godless life. He married an ungodly woman, and from the descendants of this union 310 died as paupers, 150 were criminals, 7 were murderers, and more than half of the women were prostitutes.

In contrast, the record of Jonathan Edwards' progeny tells a much different story. An investigation of 1,394 known descendants of Jonathan Edwards revealed
- 13 college presidents,
- 65 college professors,
- 3 United States Senators,
- 30 judges,
- 100 lawyers,
- 60 physicians,
- 75 army and navy officers,
- 100 preachers and missionaries,
- 60 authors of prominence,
- 1 Vice-President of the United States,
- 80 public officials in other capacities,
- 295 college graduates.

Today, instead of the blessings like those that came to Jonathan Edwards' progeny, we are seeing a growing multitude like the descendants of Max Jukes! Have you seen a family in which the grandfather was an alcoholic – and his sons and grandsons abuse alcohol, too? Have you seen a family plagued with sickness, drug abuse, debt, poverty? Often that is because someone did not make good choices. We are going to leave a legacy for our children and grandchildren. Will we pass on a blessing or a curse?[8]

If you want to leave a legacy,
impact someone's life.

WE REAP WHAT WE SOW

In a number of proverbs, King Solomon suggests that right living is to be preferred over wickedness. He describes the nature of righteousness as being immovable and that it will stand above the wicked. The wicked, on the other hand, are not secure and will ultimately perish.[9]

Is your desire for right living rooted deeply or is it planted in shallow sandy soil that can easily be washed away? Solomon indicated that the wicked would ultimately be overthrown and perish and that the righteous would survive because their character had a root that is deep and impossible to dislodge.

Solomon tells us that our decisions matter and it is better to be on the side of the righteous than to take up with the wicked. The reasoning is the same as the man who builds his house on rock or sand. If we build on sand (evil or foolish ways) then our hopes and plans will never stand up against the storms of life. If we build on rock (honesty, wisdom) our plans will hold firm.

We will reap what we sow and if we sow badly because we have rejected or ignored what is right, the wise counsel of friends, or our own core values, we will reap the consequences. Those who think they know everything reject the wisdom of the wise and follow their own plans and schemes. It can be said that those who insist on following their own ways will end up choking on them.

> *Since we reap what we sow,*
> *choose your friends wisely.*

Lysa Terkeurst in her book, *The Best Yes* says, this about making decisions: "The decision you make determines the schedule you keep. The schedule you keep determines the life you live. And how you live your life determines how you spend your soul."

Think about that statement. You could say this truth in a number of ways – Ms. Terkeurst chose this particular description. But any way you say it the meaning is, *your decisions determine your life*. The consequences of your decisions constitute your day and your future. You are always living in the midst of the choices you make, therefore, make good choices. The consequences will determine how you live your life, or in Terkeurst's words, how you "spend your soul."

IT'S NOT FAIR

Unfortunately, life is not fair. Worrying about fairness, arguing about it, or fighting it will be of little value. Being "fair" generally means that everyone is treated equally (the concept of socialism). The issue of something being fair often tends to become more important to us when it impacts us personally. When something touches us directly, we become concerned about fairness.

But life is not fair!

If you believe that life is intended to be fair, then it's not fair to others less fortunate that you were born in America and are therefore privileged. It is not fair that you have avoided poverty, wars, terrorism, natural disasters, tyrants, dying in an accident, abuse . . .

Obviously it is unrealistic to argue it's not fair that we experience the consequences of our own poor choices, especially since we are the ones making those poor choices. If we think we shouldn't incur the result of our poor choices then we certainly should not expect to experience the rewards of our good choices. We must accept the fact that life is not necessarily fair and that "bad things do happen to good people."

Obviously, things happen to us that are completely random or out of our control. We can't control weather disasters, traffic accidents, or illness. We can reduce the chances of those problems by taking precautions when bad weather threatens, by driving carefully, and by making heathy choices. But we can't eliminate them all. In the end, we control what we can by making good choices and understand that some things in life simply are not fair.

Think about the consequences,
then choose wisely!

WHO TO BLAME

Blame is a big concern for many people today. When something bad happens, the first reaction by many is to find someone to blame. Many people no longer accept the concept of an "accident." It's become the norm to assign blame and "make someone pay." We have forgotten the definition of an accident: an unplanned or unforeseen occurrence. It is no longer acceptable to merely restore the victim to their position before an accident. Rather we think we must extract a huge monetary punishment from the other party.

Some of us react in illogical ways to consequences. The most illogical is the person who totally ignores the obvious dangers of what they are about to do and then rather than accepting the consequences, casts blame. They become angry or embarrassed and attempt to find someone or something to blame in order to take the attention off their own poor judgment.

Taking responsibility for mistakes, misunderstandings, or accidents is becoming a lost art because many children have been raised to believe they do not have to suffer consequences. If the result of some action is not good or right, they expect someone else will fix it and the boss, parent, or coach has no right to hold them responsible.

Admitting mistakes and taking responsibility is a characteristic of those who are living their best life.

MISTAKES!

What happens when we make a mistake? A mistake is not the end of the world – it's a mistake, not a death sentence! If we make a wrong choice, we must rethink the issue and select another path. We all make mistakes. The real challenge in life is how we handle those mistakes.

Statistics say that successful entrepreneurs on the average have seven failed business ventures before they finally succeed. What does this tell us? If something is not working or the desired result is not occurring, stop and change direction. Try something new.

Not every choice we make will be the right decision. Expect some failures in life and don't be overwhelmed if what you choose does not work out as you expect. If the choice was bad, wrong, or ill-advised, fix it!

Pride will often cause us to hide mistakes.

TIPS TO AVOID UNINTENDED CONSEQUENCES

No one intentionally makes bad choices. We may make poor choices simply because we did not understand the consequences. In reality, however, we may be overlooking the consequences because we want to follow a certain course of action.

Regardless of the reason, unintended or poor results sometimes occur. However, there are ways we can reduce the probability of negative results and increase the probability of positive results. Here are five tips you could adopt before making decisions:

1. LOOK (THINK) before you leap!

>Take time to consider the consequences.
>Ask yourself, "What would 'wisdom' do?"
>Think logically.

2. LISTEN to the advice of others.

>Seek out trusted friends.
>But, others may have their own agenda.

3. CONSIDER the pros and cons.

How will this decision impact me or others?
Will I be proud of the outcome?
What would my mother think?

4. BE PATIENT.

"Sleep on it" is often excellent advice.
Research as much as you can.

5. EMOTIONS often cause poor decisions.

Base your choices on facts and reality.
Do not make decisions based on your emotions.
Emotions can have disastrous impact on decisions.

TIPS I COULD USE

a. Underline, circle, or highlight the 1 to 3 tips above that you think could make the most impact if you implemented them in your life. You will revisit these choices at the end of the book in the Planning section.

b. There may be other things that you think would make a difference. Write them below:

_____

_____

_____

_____

*It is the peculiar quality of a fool to perceive
the faults of others and to forget his own.*
Cicero[10]

Chapter 3

FRIENDS LIFE PRINCIPLE

*"True friends visit us in prosperity only when invited,
but in adversity they come without invitation."*
Theophrastus[11]

Your personal relationships are a key aspect of living a better life. Friends constitute a large portion of time in our lives outside of work and family. The choice of your friends will influence to a great extent how you spend your time. Choosing *good friends* will have a major impact on your ability to live a better life, because in many cases they are living it along with you. If your ability to discern the character of potential friends is limited or not your strength, you can suffer the consequences of associating with people who don't really care about you.

*"The better you are at surrounding yourself
with people of high potential,
the greater your chance of success."*
John C. Maxwell[12]

This book focuses on choosing friends and the nature of the friends you want to choose. We will examine why the choice of your friends may be one of the most important things you do. Choosing good friends is one of the cornerstones of living a good life. You don't really have any control over who your family or your co-workers are, but you do determine who you call "friend."

An important component of having a circle of good friends is eliminating those who are causing you grief, taking up all your time, or influencing you to make poor decisions. Making poor choices can derail all hope of being successful, having good relationships, and achieving personal and business goals.

Friends and acquaintances have great influence over how you spend your time and what you think and talk about. What you think and talk about will determine what you do. Thus, if you think and talk about drinking, drugs, and wild parties, guess what you are likely to be doing?

The people you associate with can lead you down paths you do not want to travel. Therefore, if you want to live a better life, it's possible that you may have to eliminate some people from the group you currently think of as "friends."

Ultimately you must choose friends carefully and eliminate those who do not share your core values and interests. That may sound harsh, but it's true, because of the importance and influence of our friends.

When a close acquaintance fails any of the basic requirements for friendship, it will be very difficult for a friendship to be restored. Therefore, we must be careful not to make decisions that would hurt or betray our friends.

Woodrow Wilson implied that friendship is the only thing that holds the world together.[13] Why would he say that? He recognized that we are social animals who do not thrive in isolation. The family unit provides both the procreation of the race, and community, but we need more than just family.

We need people around us to provide a sense of well-being, protection, and community. Outside the family community our circle of friends can be our life support, particularly if strong family relationships are not present.

Tonny Rutakirwa has said, "No matter whether you believe this or not, your friends command a major proportion of your destiny; they contribute largely to your future. Choose the right friends and keep yourself around like-minded people.[14] W. Clement Stone confirms this concept with the observation, "Be careful the friends you choose – for you will become like them." Thus, friends can impact our destiny.[58]

We believe that choosing good and loyal friends is the fundamental characteristic of one who desires to have supportive personal relationships. Therefore, it is one of the five Primary Life Principles:

FRIENDS LIFE PRINCIPLE:

Choose your friends wisely.

The Primary Life Principles are to living your best life as a foundation is to a house. Honesty, integrity, and truth are the cornerstones of the Primary Life Principles. If one's life is not built on honesty it will be very difficult to end up with a life that is in balance. If you make poor choices of friends, it may be difficult to keep your house settled on its foundation. Even if integrity is one of your core values, bad relationships can destroy your attempt to live a good life.

It is our belief that choosing friends wisely is of critical importance. If you adopt or claim the Friends Life Principle for your life, you can make great progress toward improving your life. Having good friends is a gateway to enjoying life to the fullest. You will never be able to achieve your objectives if you have friends who pull you down or hold you back. Some people you consider friends can even wreck your life if they pull you into their web of poor life decisions.

Knowing your true friends is very important because it's easy to be led astray by those who are not really true friends. Those who help you clean up the messes you create are the people you want to welcome into your inner circle. There may be others who consider themselves your friends, but if they do not have your best interests at heart, don't let them influence your decisions. True friends will help you make the decisions that are right for you.

Let me repeat, they will help you make choices that are "right for you." True friends are not necessarily people who agree with you. They will tell you what you need to hear even if they know you are not going to like it. These friends are to be treasured. They protect you from making serious errors in judgment.

"No medicine is more valuable, none more efficacious, none better suited to the cure of our temporal ills than a friend to whom we may turn for consolation in time of trouble, and with whom we may share happiness in time of joy." Aelred of Rievaulx[15]

Counterfeit friends are not real or genuine and can cause you more harm and heartache than a dozen enemies. Why? You know who your enemies are and you can usually see them coming. You are prepared for trouble from your enemies, but difficulties that arise from false friends can sneak up on you and you without warning.

Ralph Waldo Emerson has said, "The glory of friendship is not the outstretched hand, not the kindly smile, nor the joy of companionship: it is the spiritual inspiration that comes to one when you discover that someone else believes in you and is willing to trust you with a friendship."[57] The real "glory" comes in knowing they have your back if something unseen goes awry.

Friends, acquaintances, and associates are all great in the good times, when things are going smoothly. The real test of friends is to observe their response in those days when trouble explodes around you and you need someone you can trust.

Choose friends wisely.

DESIRABLE CHARACTERISTICS IN FRIENDS

- They enjoy life (do not grumble and find fault with everything).
- They have a pleasing personality.
- They are better than me!
- They make me feel good about myself.
- They challenge me to be the best I can be.
- They have interests similar to mine (art, music, sports, religion, hobbies, life goals, etc.).

TIPS YOU COULD USE

a. Underline, circle, or highlight the desirable characteristics above that you think would be most important to you. You will revisit these choices at the end of the book in the Planning section.

b. There may be other characteristics that you think would be particularly attractive for you. Write them below:

_____

_____

_____

_____

CHAPTER 4

Who Is Your Friend?

"Friends should be like books, few, but hand-selected"
C. J. Langernhoven[16]

MERRIAM-WEBSTER defines a friend to be a person whom you like and enjoy. It is someone you trust who will help and support you. These are people you choose to love and trust, and with whom you develop very close relationships. This would be in contrast to an acquaintance who is someone you know, but not a friend. A third category is associates. These are people who are associated with you through some special activity like work, church, hobbies, or community service.

A British publication once offered a prize for the best definition of a friend. Among the thousands of answers received were the following:

- "One who multiplies joys, divides grief, and whose honesty is inviolable."
- "One who understands our silence."

- "A volume of sympathy bound in cloth."
- "A watch that beats true for all time and never runs down."

The winning definition read: ***A friend is the one who comes in when the whole world has gone out.***[17]

How would you describe a friend? Your answer will probably vary depending on the number and quality of the individuals you currently count as friends. Friends who have been around for a while know all about you. They know your strengths as well as your weaknesses. They know what will push your buttons. They have seen you at the top of the mountain and probably in the deepest of valleys. And, they are still your friend. They love you in the good times and the bad – because they are truly your friend.

You need people of high character to fill these relationships. They must have standards or core values similar to your own or a lasting relationship is normally not possible. For example, if both parties do not have similar views about truth telling, it will be very hard to maintain a relationship if one of the parties is frequently telling lies and cannot be trusted. A real friend is absolutely truthful, even when the truth hurts.

A friend is someone with whom you can share your inner thoughts, concerns, hopes, and fears. If both parties cannot maintain confidentiality, that relationship will not endure. History and experience demonstrate that breaking confidences is almost always found out and the people and relationships involved suffer for such behavior.

There are many attractive attributes you should look for in friends but the most important is "trust." Your friends must be faithful and loyal to the relationship. If they are not, they must soon be replaced by those that are more attractive companions.

WHAT ARE TRUE FRIENDS?

Below is an excellent list of the characteristics of true friendship. When we discuss a true friend in this chapter we are referring to the kind of person described below. Therefore, associates, acquaintances, neighbors, and even family are not necessarily true friends. You may call them friends, but if they cannot be described by the following traits, they are not true friends:

- Friends really listen.
- Friends love unconditionally and forgive easily.
- Friends speak truth even when it's difficult.
- Friends are helpful, loyal, and encouraging.
- Friends see you at your worst and still love you.
- Friends enjoy each other's company.
- Friends celebrate wins.
- Friends support you during a loss.
- Friends share joy and fun.
- Friends know you better than you know yourself.
- Friends sacrifice for one another.
- Friends stick together through good times and bad.[18]

"True friendship comes when the silence between two people is comfortable."
David Tyson[19]

TIPS YOU CAN USE.

a. Underline, circle, or highlight the 1 to 3 traits above that you think are most important to you in choosing friends. You will revisit these choices at the end of the book in the Planning section.

b. There may be other things that you think are very important. Write them below:

_____

_____

_____

_____

TIPS FOR CHARACTER TRAITS YOU DESIRE

Thomas Aquinas said, "There is nothing on this earth more to be prized than true friendship."[20] You may have only a few people who you consider true friends. Treasure those people because they are worth their weight in gold. They will stand with you in victory but they will also sit with you in sorrow.

In describing friends, Richard E. Goodrich said, "Friends are those crazy people who keep coming back, in spite of being exposed to the real you."[21] You might consider that to be an amazing statement if you never had any true friends.

Why does Goodrich refer to these people as crazy? Goodrich knows it's similar to a husband and wife who love each other regardless of the unfortunate things that might be said at a time when their words should have been more considerate. Love doesn't cease to exist or friendship evaporate because someone makes a bad choice. Friendship recognizes it as a bad choice and forgives.

A true friend relationship does not develop in a few weeks or even months. A true friendship is developed and cultivated over a period of time and is always growing, progressing, and improving. Once established it can exist for a lifetime, even if many miles intervene.

> *"Friends are those rare people who ask*
> *how we are and then wait to hear the answer."*
> Ed Cunningham[22]

FRIENDSHIP IS UNCONDITIONAL

True friends care about you under all conditions. They care about you unconditionally, which means there are no restrictions on the relationship. Real friends are those people who love and care for you without thinking about it. They do not limit their concern for your well-being. They will come to your aid whenever you need it, often without being asked.

Your group of friends may be large or small. They may be new or old. But if they are true friends they love you unconditionally. They have made the choice to accept your faults and all the inappropriate things you do. They accept your foibles just as they enjoy your virtues. They like you for who you are and they will support you even when you are not very likable. That's really amazing, isn't it!

Good friends don't stop to think about whether you are in the right or in the wrong. They think about how they can help you. They care about you and want the best for you.

Does that mean they approve of everything you do? Absolutely not! If you do something that violates your values or theirs, they will not agree with you and they may be very vocal about how they feel about your actions (because they love you). But that will not alter their friendship.

Is the relationship always wonderful? Not necessarily. They may be very hurt or disappointed in your words or actions, but if they are true friends they will tell you that you are wrong or have acted badly. They may need time for wounds to heal, but they will not leave your circle just because you made some poor choices. We all make mistakes and there may come a time when you need to provide the same loyalty and forgiveness to them.

"A false friend and a shadow attend
only while the sun shines."
Benjamin Franklin[23]

Chapter 5

HOW DO FRIENDS ACT?

"Real friendship is shown in times of trouble;
prosperity is full of friends."
Euripides[24]

FRIENDS HELP CLEAN UP YOUR MESS

Friends are there when it gets messy.

"Life is kind of like a party. You invite a lot of people, some leave early, some stay all night, some laugh with you, some laugh at you, and some show up really late. But in the end, after the fun, *there are a few who stay to help you clean up the mess*. And most of the time, they aren't even the ones who made the mess. These people are your true friends in life. They are the only ones who matter."[25]

I agree with the quote above – except for the last sentence. Many people who travel through life with us matter. They are not all true friends but that doesn't mean they don't matter. They may be important for a season,

49

and then move on. Casual friends or acquaintances can enrich your life in many ways. Not everybody will be or can be a true friend. But the main point of the quote is true: the real friend is a treasure because they stay with us in the bad times and help us get on the right road again – in other words, clean up the mess. True friends are often the critical factor in restoration and recovery during the dark days of our lives.

Most of us have only a few really true friends. There may be others who are close friends, but one person is very fortunate to have more than two or three. Cultivate and protect your true and close friendships because they will be extremely valuable to you.

True friends are people with whom you dare to be yourself. You can expose your soul with them. They want you to be real, who you really are. You do not have to be on your guard. You can say what you think, as long as it is genuinely you. Friends understand the contradictions in your nature that may lead others to misjudge you.

With a friend you breathe freely and easily. You can have your little vanities, admit your envies, and expose your ridiculous habits with true friends. In opening your heart and soul to friends, these odd character traits are dissolved in the giant ocean waves of their friendship and loyalty. They understand. You do not have to be careful.

In addition, you can remain quiet in their presence. You can weep with them, sing with them, laugh with them, and pray with them. Through it all they see, know, and love you. What is a friend? I repeat . . . "a person with whom you dare to be yourself."[26]

IN TIMES OF TROUBLE

Friends are often most needed in times of trouble because you can depend on their help and guidance. They are there to give advice, offer a shoulder to cry on, and encourage you.

> *"Real friendship is shown in times of trouble;*
> *prosperity is full of friends."*
> Euripides[27]

A true friend is a friend during good times and bad, and most needed when times are not easy. Friends will challenge you, speak truth to you, and help you grow. If you have friends you could describe in this way, make sure you continue to honor and respect their friendship.

If you do not have friends like this, you may want to consider dropping some relationships and start looking for a new source of friends and associates. This is not easy but may be absolutely necessary for you if you do not have friends you can trust to support you when your life is in chaos.

False friends will leave you when times get tough. But you can depend on true friends to be there when life gets difficult. They may only provide a listening ear, but the essential need is covered because they are there, whether you cry, scream, mope, or just remain silent.

> *"False friends leave you in times of trouble."*
> ~Aesop[28]

FOOLS

Because we will refer to "fools" at various points in this book, we want you to understand what we mean by the term. MERRIAM-WEBSTER defines a fool as:

- A person who lacks good sense or judgment.
- A stupid or silly person.
- A person lacking in prudence, insight, and discernment.
- Someone who is easily duped.

The fool in this book is not stupid, but rather absurd. He is one who does not reason well or think logically. He may reason but his reasoning produces the wrong actions. He is one without a number of good character traits. Therefore, fools are often described as:

1. hating knowledge,
2. complacent or lazy,
3. hating correction,
4. quick to quarrel, and
5. Trusting only in themselves.

Given these descriptions of a fool it is easy to visualize what happens to those who are friends with, rely on, or consult with a person with these character traits. A relationship with a fool might be described as follows:

- It would be a difficult relationship because they could not trust or depend on this person.

- They would be at odds frequently because they would not see eye-to-eye on issues or solutions.

- Logic and reason would have little impact on the fool's thinking, creating difficulties in communication.

NOTE: There are many varieties of fools. Not everyone is a total fool. However, wise sayings usually assume a total fool in order to make a point.

FOOLS AND EVIL PEOPLE

It will be important to ignore fools and evil people in your midst. Don't listen to them or follow their advice because it will produce nothing that is good. Abraham Lincoln has said, "By the fruit the tree is to be known. An evil tree cannot bring forth good fruit."[29]

Don't expect people without character to come to your aid. True character is demonstrated by what you do, not by what you say. False friends will become known by their sour fruit. They will not be there when needed and their advice may be more self-serving than helpful to your situation.

> *"On stupidity – there is no such thing as a foolproof plan. If there are fools about, no plan is proof against them."*
> Marsha Hinds[30]

Don't associate with fools. Don't travel with them, don't eat with them, stay completely away from them. They will suck you into their web of trouble and drain you dry. Don't be tempted by their lies and promises. Don't allow them to talk you into participating in their unproductive ways or crazy schemes.

If you have certain things that are temptations in your life and your associates want to expose you to such activities, run from them. Their goal is to entice you or lure you into their circle. Why? Misery loves company. Their schemes or temptations will lead you down a path that will be difficult to reverse. You can get in over your head very quickly and soon be overwhelmed by your circumstances. Say no to unethical, unlawful, unrighteous, and foolish people.

There are many levels of evil and wickedness. Some temptations may seem minor and harmless. The problem with evil is that it can start very innocently and escalate into deep trouble in a very short time. You may think that you will be strong enough to resist when the time comes. Unfortunately that's what most people thought when they first started down the same path of addiction, pride, sexual immorality, dishonesty, etc. The result is often disgrace and guilt.

ENVY

"Do not overrate what you have received,
nor envy others. He who envies others
does not obtain peace of mind."
Buddha[31]

Envy in and of itself is not an attractive characteristic. But envy of wealth, possessions, power, or foolish people is particularly dangerous. Don't allow others to talk you into anything because you envy their possessions or their position. If you envy people then you typically want to be like them or do what they do. If you begin to associate with undesirable people because they seem to have something you want, be assured they are not going to give it to you unless you give them something they want. Nothing is free in the world of envy.

In particular don't choose friends based on their possessions. Malcolm X hit the nail on the head when he said, "Envy blinds men." Envy throws up walls that prevent one from seeing or understanding reality. Then pictures appear on those walls of all sorts of attractive temptations. Be on your guard against envy.

> *"Envy blinds men and makes it impossible for them to think clearly."*
> Malcom X[32]

TEMPTATION

Giving into temptation often leads to destruction. William Shakespeare is quoted as saying, "Temptation is the fire that brings up the scum of the heart." How often have you been tempted to do something that your heart told you was not good?

One of the dangers in associating with undesirable people is that they tempt you to do things you wouldn't otherwise do. If temptations are allowed to control your decision-making, they can produce unwanted consequences. Less dramatic temptations might seem more like inconveniences. It's the person who says, just have . . .

- one drink,
- one drug or pill,
- one ride home with a driver who has been drinking,

- one ride with someone you do not know well,
- one party with people you don't know,
- one hour without a babysitter for your child,
- one sick day when you want a vacation, or
- one innocent lunch with someone not your spouse,

that can change your life forever.

These activities do not send up warning signals for some people. Fools will dismiss this type of behavior because they tend to think it's harmless. "I am only going to do this once." Unfortunately that may be their "famous last words."

Even minor lapses in judgment can result in serious problems. Rather than ignoring the danger signals, we should be thinking:

- What is the worst that could happen?
- Why am I doing this?
- What is the motive of the one offering the invitation?
- Do I have any reason to trust this person or the situation?
- What would my mother say?

There is an old saying that if you lie down with pigs, you will be covered with their muck. In other words, you will become associated with and acquire the characteristics of those people you play in the mud with. Resisting evil temptations becomes very difficult if you associate with people who are prone to do things you want to avoid.

> *"The best way to resist temptation is to avoid it.*
> *Prevention is far, far better than repentance."*
> Spencer W. Kimball[33]

It's important to avoid being led into trouble by others. Likewise we should not lead others into difficult, compromising, or unlawful situations. Thinking you can be involved with questionable activity, without getting caught up in it, is the height of foolishness. If you participate in the questionable activities of your friends or associates you will soon become part of the group and those questionable activities will eventually seem acceptable.

You are living an illusion if you believe you can associate with people of questionable character and not be affected by their behavior. It may be very difficult to terminate long term relationships, but that may be necessary if those who you call friends do not have the same standards or core values as you do.

PEER PRESSURE

All peer pressure is not necessarily bad. Friends, co-workers, and team members can urge you toward goals and achievements that are laudable. Friends might strongly suggest or counsel you on important decisions. They may help you avoid making bad choices. Peer pressure can be valuable if it is motivating you toward high character and commendable results.

It can convince you to do something that violates your core values or your sense of right or wrong. Never compromise your moral or ethical standards. The result of compromising your values can result in hurt and suffering you cannot easily fix.

"No one intends to make serious mistakes.
They come when you compromise your
standards to be more accepted by others.
You be the strong one. You be the leader.
Choose good friends and
resist peer pressure together."
Richard G. Scott[34]

But peer pressure can be a serious hurdle to overcome when you are being encouraged to do something you don't want to do or know you should not do. The situation can become serious if you are threatened with expulsion from your group.

Negative peer pressure often occurs when you are being urged to do something by others who do not necessarily have your best interests at heart. You often must make a decision on the spot. If you have ever done something because of peer pressure and then later regretted that decision you understand the pressure that exists to follow the crowd or do what is convenient so as not to make a scene or lose a friend.

Peer pressure is effective because the focus is all on the one being pressured. Fear of rejection is extremely effective leverage. The one being pressured may fear ridicule from those in the group. The fear of losing status, relationships, or friends is very real to the one being pressured. In some cultures "losing face" is a terrible burden that no one wants to experience.

"Since no one enjoys losing friends or being cast out
of his own circle, peer pressure, especially during the
years of adolescence, is an almost irresistible force."
Billy Graham[35]

58

Friends will defend you against others who are trying to pressure you into something they know you don't want to do. Friends warn and support you against making decisions that are not appropriate. Really good friends might even take extraordinary measures to convince you that something is not good.

Some peer pressure is harmless and should not be taken seriously. But anything that is trying to convince you to do something you don't want to do should be rejected and ignored. I have a friend who told me about someone she knew in high school who was pressured into climbing a water tower. He fell off the tower and died! This all occurred because he could not resist the peer pressure of his "friends." The result was tragic! Can you imagine how you would feel if you were a friend and were in or around that group and said nothing to dissuade your friend?

YOU ARE WHO YOU ASSOCIATE WITH

Those who associate with fools may become a fool or at least act like one. The result is typically trouble and harm.

"Be careful the environment you choose
for it will shape you; be careful the friends you choose
for you will become like them."
W. Clement Stone[36]

This quote says everything that needs to be said. The good and the bad fact about choosing friends is that we become like those we associate with. Thus, our ability to choose good friends is of paramount importance. We must make good choices.

It is human nature to emulate the behavior of others. If we associate with kind people, we are more likely to treat others kindly. If we associate with people who are generous we are very likely to become more generous.

One can even become smarter! This does not mean that one actually becomes wise simply because you have wise friends, but you certainly gain understanding by observing their behavior and the ultimate consequences they incur. Such observations can be invaluable when you are faced with similar circumstances. You may have already seen and experienced what making wise choices has produced. It becomes second nature to act in a similar way.

Conversely, if we have foolish companions, we will tend to do similar things that may result in harm to ourselves or others. We can be encouraged to invest money when we should not. We can be talked into doing physical activity that may be dangerous for us.

If you make friends with people who exercise poor judgment, you will probably do likewise. Peer pressure can influence you to participate in all sorts of activities in order to maintain relationships.

I would love to tell you simply not to be lured into doing something you would normally not do. But in most cases that advice will not be very effective. Unfortunately, the wise thing to do is reduce the amount of time you spend with such people. You may even have to break a relationship. People and their foolish ways can wear you down until you cave into their pressure to participate. Unfortunately, after you have given in once it is much easier to participate again, and again . . .

You will be known by the company you keep!
Choose wisely.

ANGRY PEOPLE

If one of your friends has a bad temper, you have learned to walk on egg shells around them, afraid that something you say or do will set them off. There is probably nothing that will make continuing this relationship worthwhile.

Benjamin Franklin confirmed this advice when he said, "A quarrelsome man has no good neighbors."[37] Nobody wants to be around, live around, or associate with people who are angry or quarrelsome. At any time, and maybe for no real reason, they can lose control.

Bohdi Sanders has said, "Never respond to an angry person with a fiery comeback, even if he deserves it . . . Don't allow his anger to become your anger. Anger is momentary madness, so control your passion or it will control you."[38] The serious warning here is that such anger can control you.

"A quick temper will make a fool of you soon enough,"
Bruce Lee[39]

Being friends with angry people is a problem as tempers can erupt at any time. There are dangers being around angry people. It is probable that you will also become an angry person. We tend to conform to the environment around us. If our life is filled with chaos we will contribute our own anger and disruption to that chaos.

Second, we learn the ways of the angry person. If they get angry and yell at their family, then we are likely to do the same with our family.

Lastly, the things we tend to emulate are often not good. Our associates may take dangerous risks and laugh it off, either because they don't care or they don't know any better. If we copy such behavior, we may find ourselves in serious trouble, because we do care about our actions and how they impact others.

An angry neighbor or acquaintance can produce the risk of retaliation because you don't really know them well enough to gauge their possible reactions to tricky situations. You want to avoid the trouble, problems, and difficulties of others and not be trapped in a difficult environment because of the angry behavior of someone else. The problem may be very difficult to avoid or extract yourself from.

Angry people make relationships nearly impossible. Chaos reigns. Trouble will surround the angry person and put all those around them on edge. Angry people often try to enforce their will through intimidation. That's why angry people make friends with other violent people. They are the only ones who will spend time with each other.

You may be lured into a situation with some underlying activity or agenda you were not aware of. This means you must exercise serious discernment in your relationships. You must not act unwisely merely to appease someone. It is absolutely necessary to walk away from the enticements of those who are not our friends.

"Tell me with whom you associate, and I will tell you who you are."
Johann Wolfgang von Goethe[40]

SUMMARY OF THE TIPS IN THIS CHAPTER

1. Ignore fools. Don't associate with them.

2. Do not envy others.

3. Do not give in to temptation.

4. Reject negative peer pressure.

5. Spend little or no time with people who have questionable character.

6. Avoid angry people.

TIPS YOU COULD USE

a. Underline, circle, or highlight the 1 or 2 tips above that you think could make the most impact if you implemented them in your life. You will revisit these choices at the end of the book in the Planning section.

b. There may be other things that you think would make a difference. Write them below:

_____

_____

_____

_____

Chapter 6

CHOOSE FRIENDS WISELY

"It is better to be alone than in bad company."
(Unknown)

"A single rose can be my garden . . .
a single friend, my world"
Leo Buscaglia[41]

True friends accept you the way you are. They do not try to change you, improve you, or remold you, but they may warn you about poor choices. Real friends will love you unconditionally. You do not have to be perfect. They will ignore your faults and even put up with bad behavior.

Choose relationships wisely because bad people can lead you into trouble. Neighbors, co-workers, and acquaintances can easily lead you astray if you are not alert. If you are lazy, apathetic, or just not alert to obvious signals you can be in deep trouble before you know it.

"Your laziness leads you astray;
your greed makes you dumb;
your gluttony makes enemies for you."
Miriam Lichtheim[42]

64

If you naturally trust people it is easy to be swayed by smiles, smooth talk, and friendly behavior. People you know casually are not necessarily your friends because they have their own agendas. These are people you may engage with on a daily basis, but they are not people you should trust without considerable thought and evaluation. You don't really know these people, regardless of how nice they may seem on the surface.

Therefore, it is important to choose your friends wisely because you can:

- be easily swayed by the opinions of others who appear knowledgeable, friendly, or powerful,
- be impressed by outward appearances and the confidence of others,
- be fooled by somebody's "facts" and not think clearly or logically,
- be enticed by the possibility of gaining some real advantage,
- be convinced to do something bad, illegal, or under-handed because your friends are doing it,
- be fooled by the words of others because they claim to be your friend, or
- be tempted by a smooth-talking person.

It's very important to choose <u>both</u> casual and true friends wisely. Choose friends who are diligent and hard-working, who have a good work ethic. Avoid proud or arrogant people and associate with those who are humble and have a caring spirit. Avoid people who overindulge and are motivated by their senses. You want people in your life who have the same values and core beliefs as you do.

Choose friends as if you were choosing family. Be cautious of people who want to gain something from a relationship with you.

"Friendship marks a life even more deeply than love. Love risks degenerating into obsession, friendship is never anything but sharing."
Ellie Weisel[43]

True friends will not desert you in times of trouble. They will stick with you like a family member would. They will not desert you because you made a mistake. But there are dangers.

Some people may act like friends because you have something they want. If you are generous with money or gifts, allow friends to use your house, cars, or boats, the relationship may hinge on the physical gifts or monetary advantages that they gain by association. Often these friends fade away quickly when the gifts stop or when times get tough.

Select your friends carefully!

RELATIONSHIP MAINTENANCE

Friendship, just like any relationship, needs your continuing attention. Very seldom can you form a meaningful relationship without spending some time and thought in making it work.
If you have ever lost or been betrayed by a friend you will remember the hurt, disappointment, or sadness that may have occurred when the relationship ended. It is particularly disappointing if you realize that with just a little bit of effort the friendship might have been saved.

When you fail to support a friend, you very quickly realize that you made a mistake.

Think about a time when you disappointed a friend. What happened? Did the relationship survive? Could the disappointment have been avoided? Did you learn anything about friendships at that time? Maybe you have been disappointed by a friend. What did you do? How did you respond? The key is to be alert to situations within a friendship that should be resolved and take action to maintain the relationship.

If you have a true friendship, there should be a level of trust that will allow you to come together and resolve the problem. Don't allow the situation to fester and become a barrier between you and your friend. Can this be intimidating? Yes! But if this is a true friendship, it's worth the effort. Fix it.

Do you have a relationship that makes you weary of being a friend? Does the constant maintenance of the friendship wear you down or wear you out? Has the relationship become toxic or dangerous to you? If this is the nature of the friendship you may have to re-evaluate the relationship. You may need to spend a little less time with this friend until you are sure it is a true friendship.

The most difficult situation occurs when you know you must drop a friend and that friend is not ready to end the relationship. Do it gently and with love. Do it slowly if possible. Think how you might want the relationship to end if you were the one being dropped. But the most important advice is, "Don't back out of your decision."

You might start by having less contact with the person. Stop or significantly reduce talking on the phone and meeting together. But at some point you may have to tell them, "This relationship is just not working for me." Under these circumstances you should be prepared to explain the reasons.

SPECIAL ADVICE ABOUT FRIENDS

Good friends help you grow and mature. They sharpen your skills and cultivate your heart. They can make life much easier because they share in your triumphs and support you in your failures. King Solomon described the advantage of having a friend:

"As iron sharpens iron, so a friend sharpens a friend."

True friends will be interested in your well-being and desire to see you grow spiritually, mentally, and emotionally. They will provide advice and counsel that will help you grow in understanding and wisdom. They might have given you this book to read. They might expand your horizons by taking you to the opera. They might listen to a TED-Talks with you. They might join Master Gardeners with you. They are simply interested in you and your success or well-being. They want you to accomplish all of your life goals. They want you to be the very best you can be.

"Friendship improves happiness, and abates misery, by doubling our joys, and dividing our grief."
Marcus Tullius Cicero[44]

One friend is good, but multiple friends are better. There is strength in numbers. However, your list of real friends is normally limited to a small number. The benefit of multiple friends, whether casual or true, is significant. Whenever you encounter someone who shares your values and interests, it is wise to determine if it would be a good relationship to pursue. All relationships will not become true friendships, but having a number of really good people around you is invaluable.

You may have heard the statement that "A cord of three strands is not easily broken." That saying is a reference to a piece of rope that is much stronger when three strands are braided together compared to one single strand. The implication for friends is that there is strength in numbers.

Friendship is a source of great pleasure and satisfaction, and generally more is better. However for some people, one or two good relationships is enough.

> *"Friendship is the source of the greatest pleasures,*
> *and without friends even the most*
> *agreeable pursuits become tedious."*
> Thomas Aquinas[45]

FOOLS

> *"By their own follies they perished, the fools."*
> Homer[46]

Avoid fools at all cost. If you associate with foolish people you will suffer the consequences. The influence of fools can't be understated so be prepared: they are everywhere. No matter what you do for a fool, they are still fools. If you put a dress on a pig, it's still a pig! If you have foolish friends or associates, do not put your future in their hands. Homer says it well: they will perish!

Fools can't be fixed. You might be able to improve some fools but believing you can correct or improve their behavior to something near normal is senseless thinking. You simply cannot get others to change their twisted behavior if they have strong foolish tendencies. Often fools are very stubborn and will not listen to any advice about how to correct their behavior.

Picazo Basha of the Shambala Sect has said, "You can't fix every fool. You can't always get others to change themselves forthwith, either, especially the stubborn and the senseless ones. Sometimes you can only wait for the rain to pour and deplete them of denseness."[47]

If you try to teach or change a fool you are more likely to suffer harm yourself. Fools must simply be avoided and the unfortunate truth is that they usually cannot be rehabilitated. There are always exceptions, but that does not mean your foolish friend or associate is the exception!

"A wise man gets more use from his enemies
than a fool from his friends."
Baltasar Gracian[48]

There are ways of dealing with fools, but the best alternative is to avoid them altogether. Simply stay away from them. Don't copy anything they do or give them the idea you are interested in their activities. Why? Because their activities will surely draw you into conflict with them and their associates, who might also be fools. Certainly, don't share a confidence or ask them to keep something secret. They are not trustworthy.

If you have friends or associates with serious character deficiencies you should reevaluate those friendships. Even if you must be around fools, don't make them friends. Avoiding them does not mean you need to be rude, but you must diligently avoid becoming involved with a fool.

CHARACTERISTICS TO AVOID

There are many reasons to avoid fools. Here are five you want at the top of your list:

- They are often violent people.
- They tend to be contrary.
- They are often gossips and talk too much.
- They can very little self-control.
- They may have evil tendencies.

"Do not correct a fool, or he will hate you;
correct a wise man, and he will appreciate you."
(Unknown)

"One fool always finds a greater fool to admire him."
French Proverb[49]

SUMMARY: FRIENDS.

This chapter suggested some important questions with regard to friends:

1. Are you overly generous with friends? Do you have anyone in your circle who is overly generous with their possessions?

2. Is there anyone in your circle of friends that you need to drop or spend less time with?

3. Is there anyone in your circle that you are not sure you can trust? Is there anyone on whom you would not call for support if you were in difficulty?

4. Do you have any fools in your group of relationships?

TIPS YOU COULD USE

a. Underline, circle, or highlight any questions above that you think could make the most impact if you examined them closer. You will revisit these choices at the end of the book in the Planning section.

b. You may think of other things that would make a difference. Write them below:

_____

_____

_____

_____

Chapter 7

HOW TO ACQUIRE FRIENDS

A friend should be someone you like.

GENERAL

The first step in acquiring new friends is to begin with a positive attitude. Meeting new people should not be a cause for great anxiety. Yes, you want to make a good impression and you hope the person will like you, but stressing over people that you don't know very well is wasted energy. Sometime the stress of meeting new people can seem insurmountable.

All the initial process of making new friends entails is just talking to people. Have regular and intentional conversations until you meet someone with whom you connect. You can just let it happen as opportunities present themselves.

The problem for many of us is that we tend to be socially shy and the thought of meeting new people overwhelms us. In reality the people we are meeting may have the same fears. Rest assured that in normal situations most people are not overly influenced by initial encounters.

If you need to actively seek out new friends here are ten tips for making the task a bit easier.

1. Start with acquaintances.

Begin with people you know or people you have already met. This is an easy source of potential friends because at some level you know them and they know you. These could be coworkers, neighbors, or people in groups you attend.

2. Make yourself available.

Be intentional in finding ways to engage people you meet in conversations. You may be able to determine whether you are interested in pursuing a relationship by just listening to someone talk in a normal conversation. Find places and people that share common interests. It is much easier to talk about something you know about and enjoy.

3. Join an organization.

There are many organizations and clubs in cities and neighborhoods where people gather. Many of them are for the express purpose of meeting new people. Get involved with organizations where you have interests in common. This will provide common subjects for conversation.

4. <u>Volunteer.</u>

Community service offers many opportunities to meet other people who are working for the same cause. This is a great opportunity to accomplish several goals because you can meet new people while you are helping others. An advantage to this approach is that you automatically are around other compassionate or service-oriented people.

5. <u>Conversation.</u>

Seek out ways to have or join conversations with people you don't know. You really do not have to contribute much unless you are very knowledgeable on the subject. Just listening can tell you a great deal about the speaker. Once you identify people you might want to pursue as friends, look for opportunities to be in or around the groups they associate with. When appropriate, start up a conversation with the person of interest.

6. <u>Eye Contact.</u>

Make eye contact and smile. Make it obvious you are friendly and open. If you are staring at your feet or looking off in the distance, no one will approach you.

7. <u>Listen well.</u>

You can learn a great deal about people by what they say. They can indicate likes and dislikes. They can reveal things about the activities they are involved in. Their speech and tone can give you hints as to their personalities and their interests. These subjects can be your opening for later conversations.

8. Ask people about themselves.

There is no easier way to find out about someone than to ask them questions. People will see that you have a genuine interest if you ask questions, and people generally like to talk about themselves. It's a subject they know a great deal about!

9. Go to lunch.

People like to eat. Ask potential friends to join you at lunch. If you are not the best at carrying on a conversation, ask others to join you.

10. Fear.

Realize your fear is in your head. If you are the new person in a group, the others will often make a special effort to include you, so be ready to say something when the time comes. Most of them will also be happy to hear your story, so don't make them ask. Be open and genuinely interested in what others are doing or saying.

TIPS YOU COULD USE

a. Underline, circle, or highlight the 1 to 3 tips above that you think could make the most help in finding and identifying new friends. You will revisit these choices at the end of the book in the Planning section.

b. You may think of other things that would make a difference. Write them below:

_____

_____

_____

_____

WHO DO YOU ALREADY KNOW?

Our very best advice in meeting new people is to start with the people you know. These are people you have already met and with whom you have some natural connection. Maybe try to reconnect with people that you have known in the past, but haven't seen in a while. Contact them by phone or text and ask if there are any opportunities to touch base and catch up.

Look for informal social groups that interact frequently. These groups often have some common connection like school, neighborhood, work, service, or special activity. These groups can be openly seeking new people or they may be relatively private. In the latter case, don't approach the whole group, but contact a few of the people involved and determine if there are ways for you to be involved. Be very low key and wait to be invited. Just let it happen.

Work on making good relationships with the people you approach. If you are a good friend to them, they are more likely to introduce you to their circle of friends.

Accept invitations to outings, parties, book clubs, lunches, and any social situation where you can meet new people. If you want more friends you cannot be a hermit.

WHO YOU DON'T KNOW

Connecting with people you don't know often takes real effort. You can use any kind of networking sites or group organizations to meet new people. The absolute best way to do this is to find groups with whom you have a common interest. For example, if you are a gardener, join Master Gardeners. If you like to dance find a dance group or take lessons. There are usually a number of business-oriented groups, social groups, or charitable organizations in your local community who welcome new people.

Look around your community for groups that you can explore. If you're a reader, consider your local *Friends of the Library* group or a book club. Every community has service clubs, special interest groups, churches and other houses of worship. Keep trying until you find a group you enjoy. Chances are you'll find opportunities for friendship in one of them.

Another great opportunity is to take a course at a local community college. Most colleges not only offer special classes but often have workshops for special skills or information. Again, you have the advantage of like-minded people which provides for an easy conversation starter.

Online communities, forums, and groups can also provide an opportunity for meeting people. This can be a long process and depending on the nature of the group, and you may not be able to meet face-to-face if you live in other cities or states. Again, find groups where you have an interest or expertise in the subject or focus of the group. Generally, this alternative should be one of the last to try.

If you live in a small town that has one or two cafes where all the locals gather, this can be a good place to acquire local news and learn about the nature of the community.

Once you meet, someone has to be the first to speak. Just say "hello" and start asking questions to break the ice. Don't hesitate to share a little about yourself so that others will feel comfortable talking with you. Following are some suggestions for carrying on a conversation:

- Be yourself and don't exaggerate.
- Don't monopolize the conversation.
- Show genuine interest in the other person.
- Talk about positive subjects; avoid controversy.
- Don't get into an argument. It never ends well.
- Be respectful and courteous; don't judge.
- Compliment the other person when possible.
- Build the conversation on common interests.
- Ask insightful questions that have some purpose.
- Initially give others the benefit of the doubt if they say something strange. They may be more nervous than you are. Ignore it unless it becomes a pattern.

Be open, patient, and don't judge a first conversation too harshly. Someone may not initially seem like a good fit, but that may change as you get to know them. Great relationships can occur with people who don't have the same interests, same temperament, or same views. It might seem that such a person is not a good candidate for friendship, but there are some real advantages to making friends with people who have had different life experiences.

Be open about who you are and what you enjoy. If you hold back on sharing about your life it will generally cause other people to do the same. You might begin by trusting the other person with small or relatively minor things, rather than assume they cannot be trusted. If they prove worthy of your trust, you can begin trusting them with more as your relationship matures.

Make a real effort to get to know the people you are talking to. Here are some possible questions you might ask at some point in a conversation:

- Where do you work?
- What interesting things have you done recently?
- What kinds of things motivate you?
- What are your hobbies or interests?
- Have you read any good books lately?
- What kinds of things are really important to you?
- What do you think you will be doing in five years?
- What are your favorite TV shows?
- Are you a sports fan?
- What is your favorite restaurant?
- Where do you like to go on vacation?
- Do you go to church?
- Are you involved with any local service groups or social organizations?

BE GENUINE

If you want to truly connect with someone you must be genuine and sincere. You should not try to be someone you are not or mask the real you. Just be yourself. Don't worry about what others think about the way you look, the clothes you wear, or the way you speak. None of that will matter in a true friendship. The keys to friendship are common values, respect, and genuinely liking one another.

Be yourself! You will not be able to maintain a façade, so don't even try. Sooner or later it will crumble and reveal the real you. And don't expect everyone to like the real you. If there is no connection it simply means there is no connection. You certainly would not expect to like all the people you meet. The purpose in the early stages of seeking new friends is to weed out those people who don't connect with you and pursue those who do.

One of the important initial challenges is to stay in touch with people that you believe might be good candidates for friendship. Speak to them periodically or go to lunch with them. It is important to make an effort to stay in touch in the early days of a budding friendship. Once a friendship is firmly established, a natural schedule will evolve that you are both comfortable with. You might see each other several times a week or it might be every several months. Frequency is not the key. Let the nature of your relationship dictate your schedule.

SUMMARY

Remember these five important principles:

- Choose good friends!
- Avoid angry and hot-tempered people.
- A true friend will stick by you and continue in times of trouble.
- Real friendship is not built on what you can get or take from one another.
- A friend can help you grow and improve.

Don't be concerned if your offer of friendship is ignored or rejected. If you want to pursue a relationship, go slowly and see if the situation changes. Understand that there may be people who will not have the same level of interest in a friendship as you do. Don't be discouraged if this happens. Accept it and move on.

Chapter 8

Friendship Requirements

Friends show they care when you most need it.

FRIENDS

Sometimes good friendships occur easily and naturally without much effort on our part. But in most cases true friendships are difficult to develop and take time to mature. Yes, there may be a connection when you first meet, but real friendship requires an in-depth understanding of the other person and that takes time.

It is wise to consider what characteristics you want in a friend. If you have thought about this in advance you can save yourself time and maybe some heartache.

Following are some tips for choosing friends:

1. ABSOLUTE REQUIREMENTS FOR FRIENDSHIP

- They must have high integrity.
- They must not be dominating or overbearing.
- They must be supportive and loyal, even in times of trouble.
- They must be law-abiding and respect the rights of others.
- They must have attitudes, values, and morals, similar to yours.
- They must have a sense of humor and be able to laugh at themselves.
- They must be respectful of the faith and beliefs of others.

2. FRIENDS vs. ACQUAINTANCES

Acquaintances are not the same as friends. You may be around a lot of acquaintances, co-workers, and customers every day, but these are not your friends. They are acquaintances. You may call them "friends" but they are not friends as we have defined them in this book. You could describe the differences between friends and the many people around you as follows:

- Friends come to your assistance no matter what time of day you call for help.
- Friends provide active intentional help.
- Friends give honest advice and counsel – they tell you the truth, even when it hurts.

- Friends support you even after you have made poor choices. They provide help in a crisis.
- Friends warn you in advance of making a bad decision.

PEOPLE TO AVOID

There are a number of common signs that can warn you about people you don't want to pursue as friends:

- They are closed, rude, aloof, stand-offish, or negative around others.
- They do or say things that are inappropriate or embarrassing.
- They are loud, boorish, and overbearing.
- They are drawn only to rich, attractive, or influential people.
- They are counterfeit, putting on a false front.
- They lack self-control.
- They are lax with the truth, making them untrustworthy.
- They have little or no compassion for people who are hurting.
- They think they are always right and have very strong opinions.
- They have core values that change to fit their circumstances.

"If a person wants to be a part of your life,
they will make an obvious effort to do so.
Don't bother reserving a space in your heart
for people who do not make an effort to stay."[50]

YOUR PERSONAL REQUIREMENTS

List the characteristics for a friendship that are the most important to <u>you</u>:

1.

_____

_____

2.

_____

_____

3.

_____

_____

4.

_____

_____

5.

_____

_____

6.

_____

_____

7.

_____

_____

8.

_____

_____

TIPS YOU COULD USE

a. Underline, circle, or highlight the concepts in this chapter that you think could make the most impact if you implemented them as requirements for friends in your life. You will revisit these choices at the end of the book in the Planning section.

b. You may think of other things that would make a difference. Write them below:

_____

_____

_____

_____

Chapter 9

BE A FRIEND
TO GAIN A FRIEND

The perspective of the previous chapters has been primarily on your friends: how you select them, how you treat them, and how they influence your life. We have said very little about how you should be a good friend to others. If it were not otherwise obvious, we should be the kind of friend to others that we want them to be to us.

We have chosen the ten things that we deem are most important about how we should treat those we consider our friends.

TEN WAYS TO BE A GOOD FRIEND

1. Do not violate your own personal core values.

You must stand on your own core values regardless of the situation. You must never compromise your values in order to please or impress a friend. Since you want friends that have similar core values, doing something edgy is more likely to have negative consequences than positive.

Hold to your core values even when your friend might prefer you relax your standards. If backing off your core values is necessary to maintain a relationship, then you don't want that kind of friend.

2. Be trustworthy. Do not betray confidences. Be dependable and reliable.

A good relationship must be based on honesty, integrity, and truth. People of integrity do not share the intimate details or conversations they have with their friends.

Friends need to know that you are dependable and reliable. You will do what you say. You will be there when you promise to help. You will be there when needed even though you were not asked.

3. Be honest. Do not lie about anything.

As indicated above, honesty and integrity are key foundations for a healthy relationship. If you lie or tend to shade the truth, your friends will soon learn that you cannot be trusted. Relationships are built on trust.

Once it becomes clear that honesty is not important to you, it will be impossible to establish a true friendship. You must establish integrity as a common standard or a serious relationship cannot be established or maintained.

4. Be loyal. Do not allow lapses in judgment, mistakes, or emotional reactions derail your relationship. Be forgiving.

A friend is loyal. You cannot abandon friends simply because they make mistakes. We all make mistakes. Think how often you have made poor choices or said something that should have been left unsaid.

Be forgiving when your friends make errors in judgment. If they make poor choices in your relationship, speak with them frankly and then move on. Nothing will be gained by nursing a hurt that can be resolved by grace and forgiveness.

If the poor judgment of a friend involves others, offer to help resolve the circumstance if that is appropriate. Do not let poor choices or errors in judgment destroy a good relationship.

5. Be helpful, regardless of the situation. Be present whenever you can provide assistance. Participate in their activities and interests. Be aware how you can help them in areas where they are weak. Be willing to sacrifice your time and give of your talents.

If you want to be a good friend, you must be present. You must be there when you can help and assist your friend in any aspect of their life.

Do you have to be involved in all their activities? No. But friends normally have common interests, so be ready to participate in activities that you both enjoy. If you have very few common activities, then make some. That's what friends do.

We all have strengths and weaknesses and you will soon learn these about your friends. If you have strengths in areas where your friend is weak, be willing to share your thoughts, advice, or expertise. You may be able to teach a friend how to knit. If you are good at building and carpentry you can help your friend in both the planning and the building of home projects.

Remember, the enjoyment comes from spending time with the friend, not necessarily in the particular activity.

6. Be a good listener. Sometimes it is only your presence that is needed. Only give advice if it is asked for or needed.

Friends often just need people to lend a friendly ear. They need to vent to someone they trust – that can be you. Advice and counsel is often not required, so don't be over-eager to give it.

Be discerning in knowing whether your friend is venting or really seeking advice. Be sure your advice is valuable if it is given. If you do not have knowledge or experience about the particular situation, help your friend find someone who does. Answering the question, "What would you do?" can put you in a world of hurt unless you really know what you are taking about.

7. Love unconditionally with no restrictions.

Unconditional love means there are no conditions on your relationship. Your willingness to engage with friends is not dependent on certain conditions or events. You participate because they are your friend.

You love your friend through the good and the bad. You encourage them regardless of their attitude.

You put no restrictions on your relationship as a friend.

8. Be happy and gracious with their other friends. Jealousy is a terrible attribute.

You may not be the only friend! And, in some cases you may not be the best friend. That's okay. Know that having multiple "best friends" is normal. But even if you do not fall into that category, your friend is still your friend and you should treat them as such.

Remember, you are likely to have other friends in your life who might be bothersome for one or more of your remaining friends. Everyone has other acquaintances, associates, and even friends. They can all be a source of fun and delight. They might even turn out to be your best friend when you get to know them.

9. Be supportive, particularly in times of trouble, failure, grief, doubt, difficulties, and sadness.

A friend is there in all phases of life. Friends are needed particularly in the difficult times of life, but don't forget to celebrate the victories and the good times with your friends.

Hold a hand in times of grief and raise a hand when the days are generous.

10. Avoid peer pressure and protect your friend from the inappropriate peer pressure of others.

Peer pressure can be both good and bad. Do not pressure your friends to make poor decisions. But never let a friend make a choice that you know will result in heartache.

The key is to help friends do and accomplish what they want, not what you want.

TIPS YOU COULD USE

a. Underline, circle, or highlight the ways above that you think could make the most impact if you implemented them in your life. You will revisit these choices at the end of the book in the Planning section.

b. There may be other things that are particularly important to you. Write them below:

_____

_____

_____

_____

Chapter 10

Planning Part 1
Life Analysis

———

FRIENDS LIFE PRINCIPLE:
Choose your friends wisely.

INTRODUCTION

The objective of this Life Analysis chapter is to survey your life situation for information that will be used in later chapters to identify your core values, life priorities, commitments, and goals. In Chapter 13 we will formulate action steps to make choosing friends wisely a reality in your life.

If you have already read one of the other books in this series and completed the Life Analysis in that book, the questions and exercises are the same, but, your answers are about a different subject. However, some of your responses will be the same or similar and you might want to have that book handy as you complete this Life Analysis.

Most of us have never done any kind of extensive self-examination and certainly not thought about writing down the results. I can tell you personally there is much to be gained from writing them down rather than just thinking, talking, or meditating about them. It will give you a clear picture of your life and help you evaluate what you really want to accomplish.

The focus of this book is to address <u>one</u> particular topic in your life. It is not a complete life plan. A complete and detailed Life Plan is the subject of our *Life Planning Handbook*. See the "Next Steps" page at the end of this book for more information.

Our life planning process has five primary parts which we will cover in the following chapters.

Chapter 10, Part 1 – Life Analysis: What is your life situation today?
Chapter 11, Part 2 – Life Values: What is important to you?
Chapter 12, Part 3 – Life Principle Goals: What are your objectives?
Chapter 13, Part 4 – Action Steps: How do you get from where you are today to your goals?
Chapter 14, Part 5 – Ongoing Progress Review: How are you doing?

Life planning is not a difficult process. It will certainly be easier for those who have thought about these questions before. You might even have an existing plan of some kind. If so, this will be a good check on where you are and how you are doing. If you have a plan, it would be worthwhile pulling it out as you progress through the remaining parts of this book.

If you don't know where you're going,
any path will get you there!

I don't know the source of this quote but I have had it emblazoned in my brain since my college days. I think it came from one of my college business classes or textbooks. I have heard it repeated a number of times over the years, primarily because it is so true.

If you don't know your destination, then any choice of roads at all the forks in life will be an acceptable choice. It won't really matter which road you take because you don't have a destination in mind anyway. And when you get there you won't know you have arrived.

We need a purpose, a destination, and priorities so we are not wandering aimlessly through life. Even if you are not a "planning person," be assured we will walk you through every step. Knowing your path is important because:

1) Every path leads somewhere.

2) The life-road on which you are traveling, the direction in which you are heading, and your expected destination will determine your life.

3) You cannot allow apathy, other people, or chance to determine either your path or your destination.

Without purpose and direction it is difficult to make good choices. Just thinking about the questions we will ask in the following process will be helpful. Our planning process should produce these positive results:

- it will create focus, attention, and desire,
- it will cause action – doing something,
- it will begin to establish the importance of what you believe,
- it will help you make better decisions,
- it will help reduce distractions and hindrances, and
- it will motivate you.

"Friendship is the only cement
that will ever hold the world together."
Woodrow Wilson[51]

LIFE ANALYSIS – KNOW YOURSELF

The first step in any form of life planning is to know and understand where you are today. What is your current situation? What is impacting your decisions and ultimately your life today? The first objective will be to identify your present situation and circumstances. Before we begin, take note of the following suggestions:

1. During this process you may find that you draw a blank on a particular question. If that happens,

move on to the next question and return to the unanswered ones at a later time.

2. These questions relate specifically to the Friends Life Principle and choose friends wisely. If that limited scope makes it difficult to answer any particular question, then answer from a broader life perspective if you think it would be helpful. If the question doesn't apply in any significant way, leave it blank.

3. You might find it convenient to write your initial responses in a separate notebook or computer and transfer that information to this book after you have thought about it and modified it to accurately reflect your thoughts and circumstances. Regardless of how you develop your answers, keep your notes, as they may be useful at a later date.

4. Remember, you are developing a plan focused on the Friends Life Principle, not on your life in general. Therefore, your responses should be focused on that subject.

KNOW YOURSELF – Interests

INSTRUCTION: What are the things and activities you love to do? What gives you joy as related to the Friends Life Principle?

1.

_____

2.

_____

3.

_____

4.

_____

5.

_____

KNOW YOURSELF – Skills

INSTRUCTION: What are your greatest physical or mental skills and abilities related to the Friends Life Principle?

1.

_____

2.

_____

3.

_____

4.

_____

5.

_____

KNOW YOURSELF – Strengths

INSTRUCTION: What are your strengths, special skills, and passions in regard to the Friends Life Principle?

1.

_____

2.

_____

3.

_____

4.

_____

5.

_____

KNOW YOURSELF – Weaknesses

INSTRUCTION: What are your weaknesses in regard to the Friends Life Principle?

1.

_____

2.

_____

3.

_____

4.

_____

5.

_____

KNOW YOURSELF – Roadblocks

Who or what things do you fear the most? What are the roadblocks, distractions, and hindrances that might prevent you from improving your life in any way? Circle any that might apply and add your own in the empty boxes.

Disabilities	Failure	Bankruptcy	Divorce	Loss of job
Public speaking	Confrontation	War	Loss of friends	Peer pressure
Poor health	My boss	Guilt	No legacy	God
Time	Apathy	Relationships	Death	Family
Inability to stand firm	Immoral behavior	Unethical behavior	Lack of skills and abilities	Emotions and feelings
Fears and insecurities	Lack purpose in life	Lack of Core values	Lack of patience	Improper motives
Bad habits				

INSTRUCTION: Based on what you circled above, record any serious roadblocks or hindrances that could prevent you from achieving the Friends Life Principle. Indicate the reason they are roadblocks.

1.

_____

2.

_____

3.

_____

4.

_____

KNOW YOURSELF – Character

How would you evaluate your personal character? Do you have any serious character flaws (your religious friends might refer to these as sins)? If you have any serious character flaws in your life, you may need to deal with them in order to make real progress toward the Friends Life Principle objectives.

INSTRUCTION: Circle the positive traits which you lack and the existence of character flaws that might hinder your ability to achieve the Friends Life Principle.

LACK OF POSITIVE CHARACTER TRAITS:				
Honesty	Kindness	Caring	Forgiving	Goodness
Hopeful	Humility	Dependable	Loving	Diligence
Respectful	Godly	Patient	Generous	Satisfied
Peace	Merciful	Trustworthy	Self-controlled	Thankful
Devout	Disciplined	Obedient	Gentle	Prudent
Sincerity	Fair/Just	Grateful		
EXISTING CHARACTER FLAWS:				
Bad language	Boastfulness	Gossip	Slanderous	Lying
Cheating	Stubbornness	Anger	Hostility	Fear
Foolishness	Mischievousness	Rebellion	Hypocrisy	Envy
Unruliness	Ingratitude	Pride	Immorality	Addictions
Jealousy	Bitterness	Hatred	Unforgiving	Shame
Respect	Deceitfulness	Deceit	Vanity	Revenge

The above list is not exhaustive. If there are other issues you should add, write them in the empty boxes above.

INSTRUCTION: Review the issues you have identified and list anything below that could <u>seriously</u> hinder achieving the Friends Life Principle. List the issue and how it would negatively impact your ability to achieve your objectives.

1.

_____

_____

2.

_____

_____

3.

_____

_____

KNOW YOURSELF – Conclusion

This concludes your information gathering. You should now have at your fingertips a good overview of who you are and what might impact your ability to achieve the Friends Life Principle, both good and bad.

The next step in the process of knowing yourself is to use this information to determine your core values, life priorities, and life commitments.

Chapter 11

Planning Part 2
Life Values

FRIENDS LIFE PRINCIPLE:

Choose your friends wisely.

CORE VALUES

What are the standards by which you live? What values do you cherish? What do you believe in? What values or standards will you absolutely not compromise or violate? The latter are your *core values*.

Self-assessment and full understanding of yourself and your environment must begin with identifying and knowing your core values. Core values are the principles, standards, or beliefs that are so important to you that you would not violate them. They will dictate your most important decisions and help you choose your direction.

You don't need to have your whole life figured out, but you do need to know what matters most to you. You need to know your ethical and moral standards. What issues or actions do you believe in so strongly that you would be deeply ashamed if you violated them? These are values and principles you believe in and live by, and to the best of your ability you will not forsake them. They represent who you really are. They are your core values.

If you are a religious person you might have a core value that indicates you would stand firm on your religious principles, and you might name them. If you love and seek intellectual improvement you might have a core value related to seeking and gaining knowledge and wisdom. If you are a dedicated parent you probably have core values related to your children or parenting.

Core values may change or become more or less important as you age and the path of your life journey changes.

You may be aware of several of your core values but you probably have never written them down. This exercise will be an important step in understanding yourself and what is important to you.

If this is a new subject for you, you might start by looking at all the topics on the "Life Planning Series" page (prior to Chapter 1) and determine if any of those subjects represent core values for you. There are other subjects that might be appropriate for you to consider, for example: wisdom, influence, health, leadership, security, fitness, family, volunteer service, ethics, joy, relationships, moderation, balance, justice/injustice, addictions, laws, safety, etc.

Your core values should cover the things that are important to you. For example, you might have a core value of: "I will always try to do what is right and I will teach my children to do what is right, even if it is uncomfortable." Or, you might have a core value related to money: "I will never spend more than I earn. I will pay off credit cards monthly."

FINAL CORE VALUES

Develop these values based on a total life perspective, not just the Friends Life Principle, and make them work for you. If you have never thought about this before, we recommend you begin with 5 to 8, but no more than 12. This is a critical step in this planning exercise, so spend sufficient time thinking and evaluating your final choices. Remember, core values are those values or standards that you will absolutely not compromise or violate.

INSTRUCTION: Develop your list of core values and record them here. We suggest you try to list twelve and then cut the list back to the best 5 to 8.

1. _____

2. _____

3. _____

4. _____

5. _____

6. _____

7. _____

8. _____

9. _____

10. _____

11. _____

12. _____

Do any of the core values you listed above relate to choosing friends wisely? If not, do you need one? You may not, but don't leave it off because you overlooked the obvious. You may want to include one in order to give your objectives for the Friends Life Principle more focus and importance at this time.

LIFE VALUES: Priorities (initial list)

Our perspective in this exercise is your total life, not just the Friends Life Principle.

What are the things that are very important to you <u>today</u>? What are your life priorities? Where do you <u>currently</u> spend your money and your time? What do you spend your life doing and thinking about? For this initial list of priorities, ignore anything new that you may be considering relative to living a better life. Record just your priorities <u>today</u> (the good and the bad).

If you do something daily or regularly, then it is probably a priority. If you average more than an hour a day doing something, it's also probably a priority. What do you regularly spend money on? Assuming you have a normal

8:00 – 5:00 job, what do you do in the evenings and on weekends?

You might have Life Priorities related to your spiritual life, the educational system where you live, the ethical standards of your friends, your health and diet, hobbies and activities, raising your children, your marriage, your times of pleasure and relaxation, politics, volunteer service, your work ethic, saving money, immorality, your job or career, where you will live, your personal growth, etc.

INSTRUCTION: What are your actual top 6 to 12 life priorities today? Record them here based on a total life perspective.

1.

_____

2.

_____

3.

_____

4.

_____

5.

_____

6.

_____

7.

_____

8.

_____

9.

_____

10.

_____

11.

_____

12.

_____

ISSUES – URGENCY:

If you learned that you had only two years of life left, what impact would that have on your Life Priorities? How might they change?

_____

_____

_____

_____

_____

_____

ISSUES – SACRIFICES AND RISKS:

What new risks or sacrifices would you have to make in order to accomplish the Friends Life Principle? Would that change your current Life Priorities?

_____

_____

_____

_____

_____

ISSUES – KNOWING YOURSELF:

Look back over the "Life Analysis – Know Yourself" and determine if there is anything that should change or be added to your Life Priorities.

_____

_____

_____

_____

_____

ISSUES – LIVING A BETTER LIFE:

Given a desire to adopt the Friends Life Principle for your life, what new priorities would you need to adopt? Ask yourself what you must absolutely do in order to successfully live a better life. What new priorities does that create and how would any existing priorities have to change?

_____

_____

_____

_____

_____

_____

_____

_____

FINAL LIFE PRIORITIES

Prepare a complete list below of your new and revised total Life Priorities. Try to keep this list at 6 to 8, but no more than 12. You should intentionally include priorities that relate to the Friends Life Principle.

1.
_____

2.
_____

3.
_____

4.
_____

5.
_____

6.
_____

7.
_____

8.
_____

9.
_____

10.
_____

11.
_____

12.
_____

LIFE COMMITMENTS

Are these Commitments the same as Life Priorities? No! Your Life Priorities identify the _things that are very important_ to you, while Life Commitments are _things you must do_ to make Life Priorities a reality in your life. Life Commitments are sometimes useful if they focus on areas where you have particular difficulties.

It's very possible that there are new commitments you must make that are not directly related to the Friends Life Principle. For example, if your desire is to be honest you will also have to commit to being trustworthy, dependable, reliable, and loyal. If you want to be generous, then you can't love money. If you desire to guard your speech, then you cannot be out of control and let anger control your tongue. If you are going to live a life free of drugs, then you must commit to eliminating friends and associates who use drugs.

The point of these examples is to demonstrate that if you are serious about the Friends Life Principle, then automatically there will be other related commitments necessary to be successful. You can have a commitment that says you are going to choose friends wisely, but that doesn't really provide you with much guidance. If you frequently have difficulty choosing friends of the opposite sex or people of other social backgrounds, then a commitment focused on these areas becomes a more meaningful commitment.

Try to make your commitments specific enough that they will be useful to you.

The important concept to recognize is that the Friends Life Principle may require committing to one or more other behaviors and traits that are related to friendship and may be troublesome if not an area of focus.

Since Life Priorities inherently identify your objectives, examine those priorities and determine the related commitments that you must make in order to achieve each Life Priority. The focus should be on what you must commit to in order to achieve the Friends Life Principle.

INSTRUCTION: List the traits, behaviors, activities, or habits that you must manage or control in order for you to achieve the Friends Life Principle (one or two words).

1. _____

2. _____

3. _____

4. _____

5. _____

6. _____

7. _____

8. _____

9. _____

10. _____

FINAL LIFE COMMITMENTS

INSTRUCTION: Based on the above, develop the Life Commitments you feel you should make in order to successfully achieve the Friends Life Principle. These should be significant commitments, therefore, select the 4 to 8 that would really help you choose friends wisely.

"There's a difference between interest and commitment.
When you are interested in doing something,
you do it only when it's convenient.
When you're committed to something,
you accept no excuses, only results."
Kenneth Blanchard[52]

1.

_____

_____

2.

_____

_____

3.

_____

_____

4.

_____

_____

5.

_____

_____

6.

_____

_____

7.

_____

_____

8.

_____

_____

Chapter 12

Planning Part 3
Life Goals

FRIENDS LIFE PRINCIPLE
Choose Friends Wisely

"Life takes on meaning when you become motivated,
set goals and charge after them
in an unstoppable manner."
Les Brown[53]

Our Life Goal in this book is the Friends Life Principle: *I will choose friends wisely.* A complete plan would have other goals, but in this book we are focused only on one goal of our primary principles: friends.

If it would be useful for you, you may want to note or record other Life Goals you already have or you want to make given the material you have read in this book.

Life Goals are your objectives for the future. They are influenced by your Core Values, Life Priorities, and you're your Life Commitments.

LIFE GOALS

INSTRUCTION: We have entered the Friends Life Principle goal, and you may list other personal goals, if you like.

1. *I will choose my friends wisely.*

    OTHERS (for future use):

    2.

    _____

    3.

    _____

    4.

    _____

    5.

    _____

    6.

    _____

"Your ability to discipline yourself to set clear goals, and then to work toward them every day, will do more to guarantee your success than any other single factor."
Brian Tracy[54]

Chapter 13

Planning Part 4
Action Steps

————

FRIENDS LIFE PRINCIPLE:

I will choose my friends wisely.

If you want something to happen,
you will need to take action.

INTRODUCTION

All the work in the previous chapters has given you a
wealth of knowledge about where you are today and what
you want to achieve in the future. You have even written it
down. This is the point at which you actually take the step
to determine what you are going to do about it.

As you think about what you need to do, include language
that would allow you to measure your success or progress,
if possible. Where appropriate, include the dates when
you intend to begin and complete each step. The best

action steps are those that can be measured, allowing you to easily evaluate your progress.

In most cases the Life Principle involved will dictate the nature of the action steps you will want to take. For example, if the goal is to choose friends wisely, having an action step that says, "I will choose friends wisely" is probably too general in nature. Think about specific situations or identify specific character traits you want in a friendship.

If you have a number of questionable friends or acquaintances, you might develop a list of concerns about those questionable relationships.

If your primary concern is one particular person, then only develop action steps to deal with that particular situation. When you develop your action steps, concentrate on the areas that cause you difficulty. Don't bother with areas where you don't really have a problem.

ACTION STEPS – FIRST DRAFT

Following is a list of subjects for developing your action steps. You can do all of them or just those that you expect will produce the results you want. Your ultimate objective is to end up with 4 to 6 action steps you intend to implement in your life. You will have other actions (maybe a large number) on your initial list, but the ultimate goal is 4 to 6 good steps that you are confident will have a significant impact on achieving your objectives.

IMPORTANT: Produce as many good ideas as possible in this listing process. They may be useful at a later date.

ACTION STEPS – Initial List

INSTRUCTION: Do each of the following in order to produce an initial list of actions steps for making the Friends Life Principle a reality in your life. After you produce this initial list you will consolidate and remove the ideas that are not on target. We suggest doing this initial list in a separate notebook or on your tablet or computer.

Step #1 – TIPS FOR IMPROVEMENT

You have actually done much of the work for utilizing the tips we have discussed. In chapters 3 through 9 we provided tips on how you might improve a particular character trait. You were asked to highlight 1 to 3 suggestions you thought might work best for you and to list any other thoughts you had that would improve that trait.

Go back through the entire list of tips you chose and the ideas you added and select the ones you might actually want to use as action steps. Select the ones that would have the most positive impact on the Friends Life Principle. Choose the best 4 to 12 tips, and write them in the space below in any order. [The tips are located on pages 22, 36, 42, 46, 63, 72, 76, 87, and 93].

TIPS:

1.

_____

2.

_____

3.

_____

4.

_____

5.

_____

6.

_____

7.

_____

8.

_____

9.

_____

10.

_____

11.

_____

12.

_____

CHOOSE THE BEST TIPS:

From the list above, choose the top 4 to 6 tips and list them in <u>priority</u> order:

1.

_____

2.

_____

3.

_____

4.

_____

5.

_____

6.

_____

Make one or more of these tips the first entries on your to your master list of Initial Action Steps.

Step #2 – IMPLEMENTATION TECHNIQUES

It will be helpful for you to think about implementation techniques before you begin determining your final action steps. These are techniques you can utilize to help you achieve your goals. You might automatically mentally use some of these concepts when you are developing and working your plan. But if they are not already second nature to you, they could be part of your action steps.

Be Intentional. If you are going to accomplish anything of value, change some part of your life, or achieve a goal, you will need both discipline and intentionality. Developing a plan and even writing down action steps will accomplish very little unless you actually follow through. You must be committed, disciplined, and intentionally do what's necessary.

Be open to change. Change is occurring daily all around us. If we are rigid and not open to new ways and new ideas, it is often difficult to accept good advice. How can new ways to evaluate friends, for example, help you make better choices in relationships?

Seek knowledge and understanding. We cannot afford to be ignorant. Those with skills and expertise can teach us much. Seek new understandings rather than remain in a rut because "that's the way it has always been done."

Seek help. Ask trusted friends for advice or assistance.

Have an accountability partner. Find someone to hold you accountable for the commitments and actions steps of your Plan.

Recruit a fellow participant. Find someone who is also interested in making changes in their life and travel the path together. Not only can they support you, but you can help them succeed. Your paths do not need to be the same: the purpose is encouragement, not counsel.

Maximize use of your strengths. If you are making significant changes in your life, utilize your strengths to assist in your success. You are likely to be more successful if you use your existing strengths than your weaknesses.

Make good decisions. Much of our success in life occurs when we make right, good, and proper choices. If this has been difficult for you in the past, make this one of your action steps. If you need a quick review, read the Appendix titled, "Wise Decision-Making" at the end of this book.

Apply filters. Filter out of your life people, places, and situations that create temptations that would hinder your goal to achieve the Friends Life Principle. For example, if you are fighting an alcohol addiction, you should not spend time in bars. If you are having trouble with honesty and integrity, you can't associate with people who lie and are untrustworthy.

Review the "IMPLEMENTATION TECHNIQUES" above and determine which techniques might be effective for your purposes. Include those techniques as action steps on your initial list.

Step #3 – CHARACTER ISSUES

Look back over Chapters 10 and 11 and identify situations that will make your commitment to the Friends Life Principle difficult to achieve. Also, think about actions that would make the Life Principle easier to achieve if they existed or were true. Then write out action steps that would advance your ability to make good choices in selecting friends.

> 1. What personal characteristics in the "Life Analysis – Know Yourself" section need to be modified in order to achieve the Friends Life Principle?

> 2. What Life Values (core values, priorities and commitments) require action steps in order to achieve the Friends Life Principle?

Step #4 – LIFE VALUES

What Life Values (core values, priorities and commitments) require action steps in order to achieve the Friends Life Principle? Add them to your list.

Step #5 – WHAT IF I FAIL?

Do you need any action steps relative to what you will do if something fails? Think in advance what you will do if you have a temporary lapse or failure of some kind. For example, if your goal is to choose friends carefully, what will you do if you make a bad choice? What will you do if you already have a toxic friendship?

If you decide not to add an action step for this issue, think about the possible situations in advance and know what you are going to do if they occur.

Step #6 – BRAIN STORMING

If you aren't satisfied with your list, try to think of other options. If you can't do that on your own, get a few friends to help you brainstorm the topics on which you need more input. The purpose here is to accumulate ideas, not evaluate them. You will do the evaluating later. Seek any kind of ideas! Often one seemingly crazy idea leads to a very good one.

Step #7 – CULL AND CONSOLIDATE

You should have a substantial list of steps and ideas after doing all of the above. Now it's time to finalize your initial list.

1. Reduce the list to the good and workable ideas. Remove anything you do not want to keep on your list.

2. Eliminate or combine the duplicates into similar groupings or headings.

3. Consolidate the similar ideas into one. You may want to have sub-points for the larger ideas.

4. Prioritize the groups. Within each group, prioritize the ideas.

5. Save this list permanently.

EXAMPLES

Your list might include statements like:

> a. I will intentionally try to make friends with people that share my love of _____.

> b. I will not make choices based totally on the opinions of others. I will independently come to my own conclusions.

> c. Before pursuing a closer relationship with _____, I will confirm that they hold the same core values as I do.

> d. I will significantly reduce my interactions with _____, with the intention to ultimately sever this relationship.

LIFE PLANNING ADVICE

GENERAL

Depending on your circumstances, reevaluating your friendships can be challenging and require courage on your part. Don't give up if the road gets a bit bumpy. Stay committed to your core values, set aside your emotions, and make the hard choices required.

If relationships have historically been a problem for you, it may be scary to undertake changes that might be disruptive in your life. But it is necessary to be bold and decisive when it comes to choosing the right friends. Being bold does not mean you should be insensitive. Be diligent and steadfast in achieving your goal of choosing your friends wisely.

KEY TO SUCCESS

We believe that a key attribute for success is patience and perseverance. Assuming you have a real desire to make changes, you must be honest with yourself and honest in your evaluations of your friends. When you have made the hard choice of moving away from a relationship, do it with grace and class. Be sensitive to the feelings of the other person, but be steadfast in your decision.

FINAL ACTION STEPS

SUBJECT: **Friends**

GOAL: **To Choose Friends Wisely**

FINAL ACTION STEPS:
Choose the 4 to 6 best action steps from your initial list and enter them below

1.

_____

_____

_____

2.

_____

_____

_____

3.

_____

_____

_____

4.

_____

_____

_____

5.

_____

_____

_____

6.

_____

_____

_____

<u>TECHNOLOGY:</u> Consider entering information or reminders on your phone, tablet, or computer.

REVIEW

Before you finalize your Action Steps, you should step back and take a broader look at what you have prepared.

1. CORE VALUES & PRIORITIES: Are your action steps consistent with your core values and revised life priorities?

_____

_____

2. FAMILY: Are your action steps consistent with your family's expectations?

_____

_____

    a. Do you need to tell any of your family members about your plans?
    b. Do you want to ask a family member for help?
    c. Will anything you do in this plan impact a family member? If so, you may need to talk with them before you start.

3. PERSONAL COMMITMENT: Are your action steps consistent with your desires and commitments? Are you ready to make these changes? Are you missing anything?

_____

_____

Go back and modify your plans, if necessary.

GETTING STARTED

If you are excited and ready to begin, go for it! Begin with any or all of the above action steps.

But if you have any fear or reluctance, start slowly. There is absolutely no reason to try to do everything at once. Choose the action step that you think will be the easiest to achieve and get started. When that is implemented, choose the next easiest action step, and proceed through the list in that manner.

Some people may have a preference to do the most difficult one first and get that out of the way. That's fine if that works for you, but if this is going to create significant change in your life, we recommend you start slowly.

LIFE PLANNING COACHING ASSISTANCE

If you would like help completing your plan, see Appendix C, or go to www.lifeplanningtools.com/coaching, or scan the QR code below.

Chapter 14

Planning Part 5

Ongoing Progress Review and Evaluation

FRIENDS LIFE PRINCIPLE:
Choose Friends Wisely.

"The life which is unexamined is not worth living."
Socrates[55]

FREQUENCY:

During the first eight weeks, review your plans weekly. In fact, as long as you have a significant list of action steps to accomplish you should take time weekly to evaluate your progress. At some point you can move to every two weeks and then monthly. As long as you still have things you want to implement, you should review your plan monthly.

We recommend you put this review time on your calendar and allow 90 minutes for your first review and update.

Based on the time needed for your first review you can schedule future reviews.

SUCCESS:

Review your plan for success and failure. What can you discontinue, what should you add, and what have you achieved? Think particularly about your goals and priorities. How are you doing? Are you making progress?

MODIFICATION:

What can be removed because it has been successfully implemented? What is not working? What needs to be changed? What other action steps or ideas did you set aside when you developed your initial list? Should any of these ideas be added you your plan?

Make the necessary changes and tell a friend about your successes!

Check List

If you like to use check lists in completing tasks we have included a check list in Appendix D that lists all the steps in completing your Plan.

Chapter 15

Implementation Techniques

FREE BONUS CHAPTER

At this point you have completed your plan, including 4-6 action steps and you are ready to begin. If you want a little more help getting started, download a free bonus chapter (PDF) that provides additional help on subjects like:

- Self-discipline
- Intentionality
- Choosing filters
    - Filter what you see
    - Filter what you hear
    - Filter where you go
    - Filter what you say
- Accountability partner

Go to: www.lifeplaningtools.link/techniques

Appendix A – How to Prioritize

General

What are your objectives? What's most important considering your responsibilities, plans, and goals? You will need to be relentless in sticking to your priorities. Like your life and career, your priorities change over time.

General questions to think about and guide the process of setting priorities:

- What needs to be done _now_?
- What is most important?
- What happens if it doesn't get done?
- When do you need to begin?
- What materials, resources and skills do you need to accomplish the objective?

The Process

1. MAKE A LIST
Write a list of all your tasks. Identify any due dates for time-sensitive tasks. It is important to maintain an up-to-date list and also wise to keep an electronic back-up of the master list. Your master "to-do" list serves as a running log of what you want to accomplish over time.

2. ASSIGN STATUS / TIME FRAME
Assign a time frame. For example, this task needs to be accomplished today, this week, this month, this quarter, or this year. Identify the date you want to begin.

3. URGENCY/IMPORTANCE/PRIORITY
Identify the urgent versus the important tasks. Ignore

anything else unless your list is <u>very</u> short. Choose one of the following methods:

a. Scale Method: On a scale of 1 to 10 (or 1 to 100) assess value or importance.

b. Other Simple Strategies

- Do the most important task first.
- Do the most impactful task first.
- Complete one major task at a time.
- Do a simple high/medium/low assignment.

4. FLEXIBILITY

Be flexible. Situations and circumstances can change very quickly. Re-evaluate your priority list frequently. If priorities change move on to the next priority. Know when to stop working on a goal or action step. Make sure that what you are doing warrants your time.

Appendix B – Decision-Making

"Unintended consequences rush us recklessly through life, allowing no time for perspective."
(Unknown)

Making Choices

People who work at staying on their path with their eyes fixed on their goal are less likely to make wrong or poor decisions. Why? They have the advantage of thinking about choices in advance and being aware of the consequences of those choices.

There are many major decisions in life: (a) choosing friends, (b) choosing schools and colleges, (c) choosing your spouse, (d) choosing a career or accepting a job; (e) buying a house, (f) investing in a business, etc. In addition, we make many other simple choices daily, like when to get up, what to wear, whether to exercise, or what to eat.

"The most difficult thing is the decision to act,
the rest is merely tenacity.
The fears are paper tigers.
You can do anything you decide to do.
You can act to change and control your life;
and the procedure, the process is its own reward."
Amelia Earhart[56]

People make decisions in a number of different ways. Some people tend to rely on instinct or intuition. They just "feel" what the right thing is to do. Others gather data and information, filling notebooks with everything they can think of that would help determine the right decision.

Some make a check list of every question and answer before they decide. Finally, there is the trusted "pros and cons" approach.

We tend to favor an analytical approach to making important decisions. It requires looking at a number of different questions before making a decision. Some of these issues and questions will not apply to every question or to your particular situation. Just ignore those; they may be useful at a later time on another question or issue.

METHOD: Short and Sweet

I know there are some of you who want to make this process short and sweet. If you are one of those people, the following seven questions may be adequate for you to make a good decision.

1. Do I want to do it or not do it?
2. Would it violate a law or a precept of God?
3. Does it violate my integrity in any way (or my core values)?
4. Would it damage my reputation, if known?
5. Would it impact others or be hurtful to anyone in any way?
6. If I can answer all the above "no," then what are the pros and cons?
7. Weigh the pros and cons, then ask, "What is the best alternative?"

TEN STEPS TO GOOD DECISIONS

1. DEFINE IT: Obtain *all* the necessary information and state the question or problem in a simple, understandable, clear sentence or two.

2. LEGAL or ETHICAL: Does this decision involve any (a) legal issues, (b) ethical standards, (c) moral boundaries, or (d) company rules and policies? Clarify in detail.

3. CONSEQUENCES: What are the consequences? Can I live with them? Who and what will be affected, influenced, or impacted?

4. RISKS and REWARDS: What are the risks and rewards? What can I gain or lose? Are the risks reasonable?

5. EXPERTISE: Do I have the knowledge, skill and wisdom to make this decision?

6. ADVISORS: Seek out advisors to provide intelligent and honest advice.

7. PERSONAL CONSIDERATIONS: Does this fit my spiritual standards? Is it consistent with my core values and life goals? Do I have a passion or vision for this issue or project? Are my motives right? Am I being influenced by feelings, emotions, fears, or insecurities?

8. ALTERNATIVE SOLUTIONS: Take time to fully analyze the information in order to make a fully informed decision from analyzing several viable alternatives.

9. DECIDE: Verify the facts, think about and study the solution, and make the decision.

10. AFTERWARD: Your work is just beginning! Now that the decision is made, monitor the situation closely so that the intended result occurs. Take corrective action as needed.

You can obtain a FREE expanded version of this Appendix! It's 20+ pages and will provide a detailed outline of how to make wise decisions.

Go to www.lifeplanningtools.link/howtodecide for your free PDF copy, or scan the QR code below.

Get a Kindle ebook version for $0.99 at:

www.amazon.com/dp/B09SYGWRVL

Appendix C

Life Planning Series Coaching Assistance

NOTICE: Go to <u>www.lifeplanningtools.com/coaching</u> for details on the nature, cost, and availability of our Coaching Assistance.

At times we all need some help making a plan, getting motivated, or being held accountable. If you want that kind of assistance, please contact us. A general overview of our offering follows.

What We Will Do: We will provide help, guidance, and encouragement in:

1. Completing Part 1 – Knowing Yourself.
2. Completing Part 2 – Core Values, Priorities, and Commitments.
3. Completing Part 4 – Action Steps.
4. Completing all Parts 1-4.
5. Completing your Action Steps.

What You Need to Do.

Go to www.lifeplanningtools.com/coaching and complete the Application Form.

How Does It Work?

We will contact you to discuss our ability to assist you and give you any details you need in order to make a decision for our help. If you become a client, we will set up a schedule to talk with you by phone or Zoom.

How Long Does It Last?

As long as you desire. You may terminate our help at any time. See the website for details.

What Will It Cost?

Go to www.lifeplanningtools.com/coaching for details.

Appendix D – Check List

If you like to use check lists in completing tasks, we have included a
check list that lists all the steps in completing the Plan.

Chapter 10: Planning Part 1 – Life Analysis, Know Yourself

☐ List the things and activities you love to do.

☐ List your greatest physical or mental skills and abilities.

☐ List your strengths, special skills, and serious passions.

☐ List your weaknesses.

☐ List any roadblocks, distractions, or hindrances that might prevent
   you from implementing the Friends Life Principle.

☐ List any serious character flaws.

Chapter 11: Planning Part 2 – Life Values

☐ List your final 5 to 8 Core Values.

☐ List your top 6 to 12 Life Priorities today.

☐ How would your Life Priorities change if you knew you had only
   two years to live?

☐ How would the Friends Life Principle or any new objectives
   change your current Life Priorities?

☐ How should the Life Analysis in Chapter 10 change your Priorities?

☐ Given the Friends Life Principle, what new priorities would you
   need to adopt?

☐ Prepare a final list of your revised Life Priorities. Aim at 6 to 8, but
   no more than 12.

☐ List the existing traits, behaviors, activities, or habits you must
   manage in order to achieve the Friends Life Principle.

☐ List your final 4 to 8 Life Commitments.

Chapter 12: Planning Part 3 – Friends Life Principle

The Life Goal is: *I will choose my friends wisely.*

Chapter 13: Planning Part 4 – Action Steps

☐ Select and list of the best 4 to 10 tips. The tips are located on
     pages 22, 36, 42, 46, 63, 72, 76, 87, and 93.
☐ Choose the top 4 to 6 tips and list them in priority order.
☐ Choose and list the implementation techniques that would be
     helpful to you in implementing your plan.
☐ Produce and list your initial list of actions steps for making the
     Friends Life Principle a reality in your life.
☐ Cull and consolidate the initial list.
☐ List action steps for those situations that will make your
     commitment to the Friends Life Principle difficult to achieve.
☐ List the existing personal characteristics that must be improved to
     achieve your objectives.
☐ List the core values, priorities, or commitments that require action
     steps in order to achieve the Friends Life Principle.
☐ List the 2 to 6 "Tips For Improvement" that you feel would be
     particularly effective for you.
☐ Reduce the working list to only the good and workable ideas.
     Eliminate or combine the duplicates.
☐ Identify and list the helpful "TECHNIQUES FOR IMPLEMENTATION"
     that warrant inclusion in your action steps.
☐ List action steps relative to what you will do if something fails.
☐ Cull and consolidate the list.
☐ Prioritize the groups and the individual actions within groups.
☐ FINAL ACTION STEPS: Choose the 4 to 6 best action steps from
     your list.
☐ TECHNOLOGY: Consider entering information or reminders on
     your phone, tablet, or computer.
☐ REVIEW:
   a) Are your action steps consistent with your core values and
      revised life priorities?
   b) Are your action steps consistent with your family's
      expectations? Do you need to communicate with your family?
   c) Are your action steps consistent with your personal desires
      and commitments?
☐ Modify your plans as necessary.

Chapter 14: Planning Part 5 – Ongoing Progress Review

☐ During the first eight weeks, review your plans weekly.
☐ Review your plan for success and failure. Make necessary changes.
☐ Modify and update your plan as needed.

NEXT STEPS

LIFE PLANNING SERIES

Should you read other books in this series? That depends on your interest and objectives. If you want to gain specific knowledge about a particular subject, then the answer is "yes." If you want to improve your life in a particular area, again the answer is "yes."

We have listed the books and the planned topics again. Please note that this list will not be final or up-to-date until the last book in the Series is published.

RECOMMENDATION: We strongly recommend that if you acquire any of the books you should also obtain _Choose Integrity_. This is the foundational book in the series. We also believe the books covering the other Primary Life Principles would be particularly useful: Friends, Speech, Diligence, and Money.

The initial plan is to publish books on the following topics:

Subjects		Life Principle
Personal Character:		
Integrity*	honesty, truth, compromise/standing firm, justice, fairness	Be honest, live with integrity, and base your life on truth.
Reputation	respect, responsibility, sincerity	Earn the respect of others.
Leadership	power, decisiveness, courage, influence, loyalty	Lead well and be a loyal follower.
Identity/Self-Image	humor, being genuine, authenticity, confidence	Be confident in who you are.
Wisdom	discernment, correction, folly, foolishness	Seek knowledge, understanding, and wisdom.

Personal Relationships:

Friends*	Friends, associates, acquaintances	Choose your friends wisely.
Family	Honor, parenting, discipline	Honor your family.
Love	Love is . . .	Love one another.
Compassion	humility, mercy, goodness, kindness	Treat others as you would want to be treated.
Forgiveness	reject grudges and revenge	Forgive others; do not hold grudges or take revenge.

Self-Control:

Speech*		Guard your speech.
Anger	self-control, self-discipline, patience	Always be under control.
Addiction	moderation, life balance	Live a life of balance and moderation, not excess.
Immorality	temptation	Set high moral standards.

Work Ethic:

Diligence*	apathy, laziness, perseverance, resilience, energy	Be diligent and a hard worker.
Trustworthiness	dependability, reliability, responsibility	Be trustworthy, dependable, and reliable.
Skills	curiosity, knowledge, education, abilities	Seek excellence; strive to do everything well.

Wealth:

Money*	wealth, poverty	Make sound financial choices.
Gratitude	generosity, thankfulness, gratefulness	Be thankful, grateful, and generous.

*The first subject listed under each of the categories above make up the Primary Life Principles.

After the initial launch the books will be published in 4 to 8 week intervals.

LIFE PLANNING HANDBOOK

If you are interested in doing a complete life plan that covers all aspects of your life, not just a specific topic of the Life Planning Series, go to:
https://www.amazon.com/dp/1952359325

SUPPLEMENTAL BOOKS

(Available after the Life Planning Series is published)

> *Daily Encouragement* (250 short reviews on topics from the Life Planning Series)

> *Table Talk* (Questions and answers for dinner table discussion)

CHRISTIAN WISDOM SERIES

Since the Christian perspective on many of these subjects is unique, we have planned a Christian Wisdom Series that will examine the Christian view on most of the subjects in the Life Planning Series. This series is planned for release after the Life Planning Series is published.

COACHING ASSISTANCE

See Appendix C for details.

Life Planning Series

The Primary Life Principles

Read these books if you want to live a better life.

LIFE PLANNING HANDBOOK	**A Life Plan will shape your life journey!** The next step in your life planning.
CHOOSE INTEGRITY	**Life Principle:** Be honest, live with integrity, and base your life on truth.
CHOOSE THE RIGHT WORDS	**Life Principle:** Guard your speech.
CHOOSE GOOD WORK HABITS	**Life Principle:** Be diligent and a hard worker.
CHOOSE FINANCIAL RESPONSIBILITY	**Life Principle:** Make sound financial choices.

Scan the Q/R code to the left with your phone to check on availability of all books in the Life Planning Series. These five will be published in 2022.

Note: the remaining 10 - 20 books in the Life Planning Series will be published individually in 4-8 week intervals following the last book above.

Go to:

https://www.amazon.com/dp/B09TH9SYC4

to get your copy.

You Can Change Your Life!

Free PDF

Wise
Decision-Making

[Get the ebook version for 99 cents]

We want to give you a <u>free</u> copy of:

Wise Decision-Making:
You can make good choices.

This book will help you make good
decisions in your life, career, family . . .

Free PDF:
www.lifeplanningtools.link/howtodecide

eBook for 99 cents:
https://www.amazon.com/dp/B09SYGWRVL/

Ebook

Free PDF

Improve your life!
Life Planning Handbook

Obtain a copy of the Handbook if you want to be guided in developing your own personal Life Plan.

Purpose of a Life Plan

- To help you develop direction in your life.
- To encourage you to make good decisions.
- To help build your life on proven life principles.
- To help you establish goals for your life.
- To identify what you hope to accomplish in life.
- To help you make the most of every opportunity.

Life Planning
Series

Life Planning
Handbook

Go to www.amazon.com/dp/1952359325
to get your copy now.

Don't wait to have a better life!

Acknowledgments

My wife has patiently persevered while I indulged my interest in this subject. Thank you for your patience.

Our older daughter has been an invaluable resource. She has also graciously produced our website at www.lifeplanningtools.com

Our middle daughter designed all the covers for this series. We are very grateful for her help, talent and creativity.

Notes

QUOTES

ACCURACY: We have used a number of quotes throughout this book that came from our files, notes, books, public articles, the Internet, etc. We have made no attempt to verify that these quotes were actually written or spoken by the person they are attributed to. Regardless of the source of these quotes, the wisdom of the underlying message is relative to the content in this book and worth noting, even if the source reference is erroneous.

SOURCE: Unless otherwise specifically noted below the quotes used herein can be sourced from a number of different websites on the Internet that provide lists of quotes by subject or author. The same or similar quotes will appear on multiple sites. Therefore, rather than assign individual quote sources, we are providing a list of sites where we might have found the quotes that were used in this book:

--azquotes.com
--brainyquote.com
--codeofliving.com
--everydaypower.com
--goodhousekeeping.com
--goodreads.com/quotes
--graciousquotes.com
--inc.com
--keepinspiring.me
--notable-quotes.com
--parade.com
--plantetofsuccess.com
--quotemaster.org
--quotir.com
--success.com
--thoughtco.com
--thoughtcatalog.com
--wisdomquotes.com
--wisesayings.com
--wow4u.com

1 Thomas Aquinas, see QUOTES above.
2 Abraham Lincoln, see QUOTES above.
3 Latin American saying, see QUOTES above.
4 Aesop, see QUOTES above.
5 SermonCentral.com; contributed by Perry Greene

6 Buddha, see QUOTES above.

7 Honore de Balzac, see QUOTES above.

8 A large number of Internet sites. Search for "Jonathan Edwards,"
  "Max Jukes," or "A. E. Winship."

9 Bible, Book of Proverbs 12:3, 7, 12.

10 Cicero, see QUOTES above.

11 Theophrastus, see QUOTES above.

12 John C. Maxwell, see QUOTES above.

13 Woodrow Wilson, see QUOTES above.

14 Tonny Rutakirwa, see QUOTES above.

15 Theophrastus, see QUOTES above.

16 C. J. Langernhoven, see QUOTES above.

17 Bits & Pieces, July, 1991.

18 Michelle Berkey-Hill, Grace and the Gravel Road, Bible Study 2/27/18.

19 David Tyson[1], see QUOTES above.

20 Thomas Aquinas, see QUOTES above.

21   Richard E. Goodrich, see QUOTES above.

22 Ed Cunningham , see QUOTES above.

23 Benjamin Franklin, see QUOTES above.

24 Euripides, see QUOTES above.

25 *41 Supremely Wise Life Lessons From Everyday People*, by Jessica
Winters, March 10th 2016, Instagram / Marisa Jarae.

26 C. Raymond Beran, *Bits & Pieces*, September 19, 1991, p. 3-4.

27 Euripides, see QUOTES above.

28 Aesop, see QUOTES above.

29 Abraham Lincoln, see QUOTES above.

30 Marsha Hinds, see QUOTES above.

31 Buddha, see QUOTES above.

32 Malcom X, see QUOTES above.

33 Spencer W. Kimball, see QUOTES above.

34 Richard G. Scott, see QUOTES above.

35 Billy Graham, see QUOTES above.

36 W. Clement Stone, see QUOTES above.

37 Benjamin Franklin, see QUOTES above.

38 Bohdi Sanders, see QUOTES above.

39 Bruce Lee, see QUOTES above.

40 Johann Wolfgang von Goethe, see QUOTES above.

41 Leo Buscaglia, see QUOTES above.

42 Miriam Lichtheim, *Ancient Egyptian Literature, Volume I: The Old
  and Middle Kingdoms*.

43 Ellie Weisel, see QUOTES above.

44 Marcus Tullius Cicero, see QUOTES above.

45 Thomas Aquinas, see QUOTES above.

46 Homer, see QUOTES above.

47 Picazo Basha, see QUOTES above.

48 Baltasar Gracian, see QUOTES above.

49 French Proverb, see QUOTES above.

50 *41 Supremely Wise Life Lessons From Everyday People,* by Jessica Winters, March 10th 2016, Instagram / Marisa Jarae.

51 Woodrow Wilson, see QUOTES above.

52 Kenneth Blanchard, see QUOTES above.

53 Les Brown, see QUOTES above.

54 Brian Tracy, see QUOTES above.

55 Socrates, see QUOTES above.

56 Amelia Earhart, see QUOTES above.

57 Ralph Waldo Emerson, see QUOTES above.

58 W. Clement Stone, see QUOTES above.

About the Author

The author graduated from the Business School at Indiana University and obtained a master's degree at Georgia State University in Atlanta. His first career was as a senior executive with a top insurance and financial institution, where he spent a number of years directing strategic planning for one of their major divisions.

In the 1990s he founded an online Internet business which he sold in 2010. He began to write and publish books and materials that led to an interest in personal life planning. This resulted in combining the wisdom of wise sayings and proverbs with life planning and the result is the Life Planning Series and the Life Planning Handbook.

The author, his wife, and two of his children and their families live in the Nashville, TN area.

WEBSITE: http://www.lifeplanningtools.com

AMAZON: www.amazon.com/author/jswellman

Contact Us

	www.lifeplanningtools.com info@lifeplanningtools.com	Website Email
Facebook	JSWellman	
	www.amazon.com/author/jswellman	**Author Page**
Life Planning Series	www.amazon.com/dp/B09TH9SYC4	
	www.lifeplanningtools.link/newsletter	**Monthly News Letter**

You can help

IDEAS and SUGGESTIONS: If you have a suggestion to improve this book, please let us know.

Mention our LIFE PLANNING books on your social platforms and recommend them to your family and friends.

Thank you!

Make a Difference

The law of prosperity is generosity.
If you want more, give more.
Bob Proctor

Have you ever done something just out of kindness or goodwill without wanting or expecting anything in return? I'm going to ask you to do <u>two things</u> just for that reason. The first will be just out of the goodness of your heart and the second in order to make an impact in someone else's life.

It won't cost you anything and it won't take a lot of time or effort.

This Book

First, what did you think of this book? Give the book an honest review in order for us to compete with the giant publishers. What did you like and how did it impact you? It will only take you several minutes to leave your review at: https://www.amazon.com/dp/1952359317

Follow the link above to the Amazon sales page, scroll down about three quarters of the page and click the box that says: "Write a customer review." It does not have to be long or well-written – just tell other readers what you think about the book. Or, just score the book on a scale of 1 – 5 stars (5 is high).

This will help us a great deal and we so appreciate your willingness to help. If you want to tell us something about

the book directly, you can email us at:
info@lifeplanningtools.com.

Give Books to Students and Employees

Secondly, do you know any schools or colleges that might want to give this book or our Life Planning Handbook to their students or their senior class?

Do you know any companies, churches, or other organizations that would like to give one of our books to their employees or members?

Here is how you can help. If you send us the contact information and allow us to use your name, we will contact the person or persons you suggest with all the details. Obviously there would be special pricing and if the order is large enough, a message from the organization's CEO could be included on the printed pages.

Alternatively, you can personally give a copy of one of our books to the organization for their consideration. We would recommend our Life Planning Handbook, but some organizations might be interested in a specific subject. If they are interested in this partnership with us, they should contact us directly.

It is not that difficult to help someone live a better life: just a little time and intentionality. Let us hear from you if you want to make a difference in someone's life!

J. S. Wellman
Extra-mile Publishing
steve@lifeplanningtools.com
www.lifeplanningtools.com

Made in the USA
Columbia, SC
26 November 2022

72105500R00089